TORAH

Made Easy

All Five Books of Moses Summarized

EPUB Version

I0834130

Dallas, Texas USA

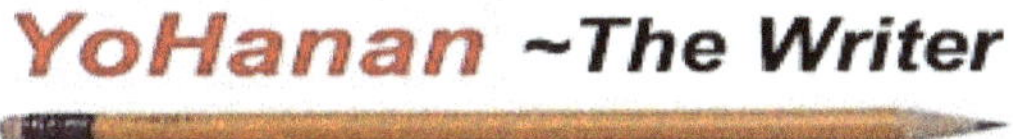

Produced, Published and Distributed by
Torah Publications Dallas Texas

http://www.TorahPublications.com
Email: Info@TorahPublications.com

This publication is for the sole purpose of spreading the word of God

Feel free to use this summary information in any way that furthers the name of God (YeHoVah) and His word. All that is asked is that you reference the **TORAH Made Easy** as the source of your information. The Torah is the basis for our life and contains all we need to know to sustain us in His grace and obey his commands.

Visit our website at www.TorahPublications.com
Printed in the United States of America
First Printing: February 2020 Torah Publications

"I call heaven and earth to record this day against you, that I have set before you life and death, blessing and cursing: therefore, *choose life*, that both you and your seed may live." ~Deuteronomy 30:19

Want to know all the stories of the Torah and Reduce the reading from 16 hours to 3 hours?

All Your Excuses For Not Reading Addressed

I don't have time to read it - It's too long - I don't understand it

I can't read Hebrew - Some of it is too boring - Why should I read it?

I thought the Torah was nailed to the cross - I'm not Jewish

Now it's Easy to follow and understand God's Words in less time

This is a great guide to use for teaching not only ourselves but others: including children. What a great way to spread God's Word

Table of Contents

Addressing Your Excuses

~for not reading and knowing God's Word, The Torah

I don't have time to read it
I would agree that reading the entire Torah would take about 15 hours for the average reader. 15-20 hours depending on how many times you stopped to reread a verse or two. Granted 15-20 hours spread over several months still doesn't seem like a big sacrifice to know God's Word. *The Torah Summary* reduces this time by about 60-70%.

It's too long
The U.S. Constitution is long too but it's the laws/rules we live by and we are all bound by them. So too are God's laws/rules. *The Torah Summary* greatly reduces the length.

I don't understand it
The Torah Summary simplifies it into easily understandable text and even explains areas that may be confusing to some.

I can't read Hebrew
The Torah Summary isn't in Hebrew. It's all in English.

Some of it is too boring
Life is boring if you let it be. If hearing God's Word is boring to you, then you need to re-evaluate you relationship with God. What if He says that hearing all your prayers is boring to Him so He'll just ignore them? The world would quickly become more chaotic than it already is. With that said, I agree some of the chapters are more interesting than others. That is the whole purpose of *The Torah Summary*. It highlights the more critical information you must know and leaves further reading to your choice. At least you will know the basics of what God wants you to know. All the chapters identify where in the Torah you can find the full text reading easily, if you desire more information.

Why should I read it?
Ah, the most important question of all. Why should I read it? Where do I begin? Well, God created the heavens and the earth in six days and rested on the seventh. He created man in His own image. He gave us (freedom of choice) a set of rules/guides to live by and said, "Today, I give you both blessings and curses. I suggest you choose life (blessings) so that you and your descendants may live." Saying this, I am assuming you already believe

in God (or maybe not), so believing in Him but not in His words is an oxymoron (a set of contradictory words, like ‘Dry rain’ or ‘Hot snow’). Both can’t be true at the same time. If you believe in God, you have to then follow His rules. Even though God gives us freedom of choice, he didn’t say there would be no consequences for our wrong/bad (curses) choices.

I thought the Torah was nailed to the cross

Not even the man called Jesus said that. In fact he said the opposite.

> “17 Think **not** that I am come to destroy the law, or the prophets: I
> am **not** come to destroy, but to fulfil. 18 For verily I say unto you, Till
> heaven and earth pass, one jot or one tittle shall in **no way** pass
> from the law, till all be fulfilled. 19 **Whosoever** therefore **shall break**
> one of these least commandments, and shall teach men so, **he** shall be called the **least** in the kingdom of heaven: but whosoever shall do and teach them, the same shall be called great in the kingdom of heaven.”

The *Torah Summary* renews for you God’s law so that you and your descendants may live. Or else you will be called the least in the kingdom of Heaven. Your Choice – Your Consequence!

I’m not Jewish

Neither is God, nor Moses, Aaron, Noah, Miriam, etc.
In the Torah, the "children of Israel" are called just that, or Israelite. The term "Jew" or "Jewish" does not exist in the Torah. Hundreds of years later, after the loss of the ten tribes, did the term "Jews" or "Jewish" begin to be used. God gave His word for all mankind for all generations.

The *Torah Summary* was written in an effort to bring God’s Word to all His people. If you do not believe that you are one of God’s people, then you should stop right here. You either believe in God 100% or you don’t believe in God at all. If you still feel your reasons for not knowing His Word are valid then God help you.

God’s commandments are not just rules; they offer us guidance and a path to a loving and fulfilling life. When we choose to follow His commandments, we open ourselves up to blessings, peace, and a deeper relationship with Him. Approach His Word with an open heart and mind, allowing them to speak to you and shape your understanding of His will in your life.

What is the Torah?

The Torah, a foundational text in Judaism, is a comprehensive document encompassing law, narrative, and ethical teachings. It is traditionally understood as the divinely revealed word of God to Moses on Mount Sinai, and it forms the first and most sacred part of the Hebrew and Christian Bible, known as the Pentateuch or the Five Books of Moses, and the first five books of the Old Testament.

The Torah is comprised of five distinct books, each with its own theme focus and narrative progression. These books are Genesis ~ Exodus ~ Leviticus ~ Numbers ~ Deuteronomy.

The Written Torah provides a narrative history of the Jewish people and outlines God's laws and ethical guidelines for living a moral and purposeful life. A central theme is the establishment of a covenant (a special agreement) between God and the Israelites (all humanity), in which they agree to follow His laws and in return, receive guidance and protection in a promised land. It contains a total of 613 commandments (mitzvot), including the Ten Commandments that are addressed in the Torah. Not all Commandments (mitzvot) apply to everyone. Some apply only to women, some to priests, some to the sick, and some to men.

How and When Was The Bible Divided Into Chapters and Verses?

Did you know that early manuscripts of the biblical texts did not contain the chapter and verse divisions in the numbered form familiar to what we have today?

Despite being inspired by God, the Bible is a collection of several short works produced by various human writers at various points in time that were eventually put together to form the biblical canon. Since the early 13th century, the majority of Bible editions and copies have divided the books into chapters, with the exception of the smallest, which are often one page long. Editors have further broken each chapter into verses from the middle of the 16th century; each verse consists of a few brief lines or words. God did not divide into books, chapters and verses.

The Bible has been translated into many different languages and versions from the original biblical languages of Hebrew, Aramaic and Greek. In fact, As of September 2023 all of the Bible has been translated into 736 languages, the New Testament has been translated into an additional 1,658 languages, and smaller portions of the Bible have been translated into 1,264 other languages according to Wycliffe Global Alliance. And some portions of the Bible have been translated into 3,658 languages.
The Old Testament was mainly written in Biblical Hebrew, with some portions (notably in Daniel and Ezra) in Biblical Aramaic, Greek and Syriac.

What are Mitzvots?

There are 365 Negative Commandments (Mitzvots)
And 248 Positive Commandments (Mitzvots)
According to the Rambam's Sefer Hamitzvos
https: //livingwithmitzvos.com/list-of-613-mitzvos/

What are Mitzvots / Mizvahs?

The Torah is the foundational Jewish text, and it contains commandments, called mitzvahs, or mitzvot (singular, mitzvah), which are the basis of Jewish practice.

At the heart of Jewish Law is the unchangeable 613 mitzvot that God gave to the Jewish people in the Torah (the first five books of the Bible). The word "mitzvah" means "commandment." In its strictest sense, it refers only to commandments instituted in the Torah; however, the word is commonly used in a more generic sense to include all of the laws, practices and customs of Jewish Law, and is often used in an even more loose way to refer to any good deed.

Some of the mitzvot are clear, explicit commands in the Bible (thou shalt not murder; to write words of Torah on the doorposts of your house), others are more implicit (the mitzvah to recite grace after meals, which is inferred from "and you will eat and be satisfied and bless the L-rd your G-d"), and some can only be ascertained by Talmudic logic (that a man shall not commit incest with his daughter, which is derived from the commandment not to commit incest with his daughter's daughter).

Some of the mitzvot overlap; for example, it is a positive commandment to rest on the Sabbath and a negative commandment not to do work on the Sabbath.

Although there is not 100% agreement on the precise list of the 613 (there are some slight discrepancies in the way some lists divide related or overlapping mitzvot), there is complete agreement that there are 613 mitzvot. This number is significant: it is the numeric value of the word Torah

(Tav = 400, Vav = 6, Resh = 200, Heh = 5), plus 2 for the two mitzvot whose existence precedes the Torah: I am the L-rd, your G-d and You shall have no other gods before Me. There is also complete agreement that these 613 mitzvot can be broken down into 248 positive mitzvot (one for each bone and organ of the male body) and 365 negative mitzvot (one for each day of the solar year).

The most accepted list of the 613 mitzvot is Maimonides' list in his *Mishneh Torah*. In the introduction to the first book of the *Mishneh Torah*, Maimonides lists all of the positive mitzvot and all of the negative mitzvot, then proceeds to divide them up into subject matter categories. See List of the 613 Mitzvot.

Many of these 613 mitzvot cannot be observed at this time for various reasons. For example, a large portion of the laws relate to sacrifices and offerings, which can only be made in the Temple, and the Temple does not exist today. Some of the laws relate to the theocratic state of Israel, its king, its supreme court, and its system of justice, and cannot be observed because the theocratic state of Israel does not exist today. In addition, some laws do not apply to all people or places. Agricultural laws only apply within the state of Israel, and certain laws only apply to kohanim or Levites. 77 positive mitzvot and 194 negative mitzvot have been identified which can be observed outside of Israel today that all can follow.

Torah Years Spanned

The years spanned in the Torah obviously overlap. In addition, the Torah is not always written chronologically, so it's not always totally clear. Nevertheless, to give you some idea, the time covered approximately in each book is as follows:

Genesis- 2,286 years
Exodus- 80 years
Leviticus- 1 year
Numbers- 39 years
Deuteronomy- 37 days
2,390 Years of Biblical History

Genesis spans more time than any other book in the Bible.
Genesis covers more time than the remaining sixty-five put together.
The Old & New Testaments cover 4,100 years of recorded Bible history.
Over one-half of it (2,286 years) is recorded in Genesis. • The remaining 1,814 years are covered in Exodus through Revelation (65 books). • 2,000 of the 2,286 years are covered in Genesis 1-11.

What follows is a compilation of the basic concepts of the Torah in a plain but essential manner. This is NOT in any way a replacement for reading the entire Torah, but a minimal rendering of His Word as an introduction to, not a full representation of its entireness. Some might refer to it as a simple, shortened, compressed, condensed, or brief version of the Torah. This is an effort to bring God's Word to His people in a shortened version so that they will better understand: because too many are not taking the time to understanding it now. We highly encourage everyone to read the entire Torah, even to your children, but until them the Torah Made Easy will give you a very solid understanding of God's Word.

The Five Book Names ~Chapters ~Verses

Names for the Five Books of the Torah
The Torah is divided into five books, each contributing to the overarching narrative and legal framework. The names in (parentheses) are the Hebrew names:

- **Genesis *(Bereshit*):** Describes the creation of the world, the beginning of humankind, and the stories of the patriarchs and matriarchs—Abraham, Isaac, and Jacob—culminating with the Israelites dwelling in Egypt.
- **Exodus *(Shemot*):** Focuses on the Israelites' enslavement in Egypt, their miraculous liberation by God through Moses, the revelation of the Ten Commandments and other laws at Mount Sinai, and the instructions for building the Tabernacle (a portable sanctuary).
- **Leviticus *(Vayikra*):** Primarily deals with ritual laws for the priests (Levites), instructions for sacrificial worship, dietary regulations, and laws concerning purity, holiness, and ethical behavior.
- **Numbers *(Bamidbar*):** Narrates the Israelites' 40-year journey and wanderings in the wilderness, their challenges and rebellions against Moses, two censuses of the people, and preparations to enter the land of Canaan.
  - **Deuteronomy *(Devarim*):** Presented as Moses' final speeches to the new generation of Israelites before they enter the Promised Land. It reviews the laws given at Sinai, introduces some new laws, and emphasizes the importance of faithfulness to God's covenant. **There are 187 Total Chapters in the Torah**

Longest Books of the Old Testament by Chapters

1. Psalms — 150
2. Isaiah — 66
3. Jeremiah — 52
4. Genesis — 50 Chapters, 1,533 verses
5. Ezekiel — 48
6. Job — 42
7. Exodus — 40 Chapters, 1,213 verses
8. Numbers — 36 Chapters, ,288 Verses
9. Deuteronomy — 34 Chapters, 959 verses
   (16) Leviticus — 27 Chapters, 859 verses

Torah Themes and Their Significance

The Torah is rich with enduring themes that have shaped Jewish and Christian thought and culture for millennia. Central among these is the concept of *covenant* (brit), the unique relationship established between God and the people of Israel. This covenant involves mutual obligations: God's promise of protection and land, and Israel's commitment to obedience and faithfulness to His laws.

Another crucial theme is *monotheism*, the belief in one transcendent God who is the creator and sustainer of the universe. The Torah consistently emphasizes God's *singularity* and His absolute authority, contrasting with the polytheistic beliefs of surrounding cultures. The concept of *holiness* is also pervasive, calling the Israelites to live a life set apart for God, both individually and communally, through adherence to His commandments and rituals.

The Torah also explores themes of *justice* and *righteousness*, advocating for fair treatment of all individuals, care for the vulnerable, and the establishment of an equitable society. The narratives of the patriarchs and the exodus from Egypt highlight God's intervention in history to bring about liberation and to establish a people dedicated to His ways. Ultimately, the Torah serves as a guide for living, providing a framework for ethical conduct, spiritual devotion, and the pursuit of a just and holy life

The Torah is the foundational work of Judaism and Christianity, comprised of the first five books of the Hebrew Bible (the Pentateuch). The word "Torah" is Hebrew for "instructions" or "teaching", and in its broadest sense, refers to the entire body of Jewish law and tradition. Some also include the oral Torah which is not the word of God but the word of man (Rabbis).

Core Content and Purpose

The Written Torah provides a narrative history of the Jewish people and outlines God's laws and ethical guidelines for living a moral and purposeful life. A central theme is the establishment of a covenant (a special agreement) between God and the Israelites, in which they agree to follow His laws and in return, receive guidance and protection in a promised land. It contains a total of 613 commandments (**mitzvot**), including the Ten Commandments.

The Oral Torah ~ The Talmud

Some Rabbis believe in and follow a Jewish *tradition*, alongside the Written Torah, that they say God also revealed an *Oral* Torah to Moses, which provides more details and *interpretations* for applying the written laws to changing circumstances. This oral *tradition* was eventually written down and compiled in the **Mishnah** and **Talmud**, which form a vast body of Jewish *wisdom*. Not all Jews or Christians accept the Oral Torah since it is man's word, **not** God's and is never mentioned in the Torah. It can be looked at as a Rabbi *opinion guide* but not as God's Law. Rules like, "You can't tear toilet paper on the Sabbath, or "You can't cut paper on the Sabbath unless you only cut it in random fashion to avoid forming any specific shape," or "dictates cutting fingernails in a non-consecutive order (e.g., thumb, middle finger, pinky, index finger, ring finger) to avoid misfortune." These are only a few of the many obscure rules in the Talmud. *Read it with caution* and common sense. Aaron and his sons were the only ones appointed by God as priests (Rabbis). All others are man appointed and thus carry the burden of misinterpretation and incorrect teachings.

Basic Summaries and Events

The Torah, a foundational text in Judaism and Christianity, is a multifaceted document encompassing law, narrative, and ethical teachings. It is traditionally understood as the divinely revealed word of God to Moses on Mount Sinai, and it forms the first and most sacred part of the Hebrew Bible, known as the Torah, Pentateuch or the Five Books of Moses.

The Torah is comprised of five distinct books, each with its own themed focus and narrative.

NOTE: When Moses recorded God's Words as the Torah, he recorded it on individual parchments (or animal skins) that were then sewn together to make one continuous long scroll. There were no book names, no chapter markings or verse numbers. Man added these much later in order to help make reference points easier. There were no sentences, or paragraphs, and no capitol letters or punctuation. Hebrew is also written and read from right to left.

The five books are: (Hebrew Name in parentheses)

Genesis **(Hebrew Name: Bereishit)**

Genesis, meaning "in the beginning," recounts the creation of the world, the origins of humanity, and the early history of the Israelite patriarchs and matriarchs. It begins with the creation narrative, detailing God's formation of the cosmos and all living things, culminating in the creation of Adam and Eve. This is followed by accounts of the Garden of Eden, the first sin, and the subsequent expulsion of humanity. Key narratives include the stories of Cain and Abel, Noah and the flood, and the Tower of Babel, which explain the diversification of languages and the spread of humanity across the earth

A significant portion of Genesis is dedicated to the patriarchal narratives, focusing on Abraham, Isaac, and Jacob. Abraham's call by God, the covenant established with him, and the promise of land and numerous descendants are central themes. The narratives explore the challenges and triumphs of these early leaders, including their migrations, interactions with various peoples, and the establishment of their families. The book concludes with the story of Joseph, his enslavement in Egypt, his rise to power, and the eventual relocation of Jacob's family to Egypt, setting the stage for the subsequent book (*The Oxford Handbook of Biblical Studies*).

Exodus (Hebrew Name: Shemot)

Exodus, meaning "names," details the liberation of the Israelites from slavery in Egypt and their journey towards the promised land. It begins with the oppression of the Israelites under a new pharaoh who fears their growing numbers. Moses is introduced as the divinely appointed leader, chosen to confront Pharaoh and lead his people to freedom. The narrative vividly describes the ten plagues inflicted upon Egypt, culminating in the Passover, which marks the final plague and the Israelites' exodus.

Following their departure from Egypt, the Israelites experience the miraculous crossing of the Red Sea and their subsequent journey through the wilderness. A pivotal event in Exodus is the revelation of the Torah at Mount Sinai, where God delivers the Ten Commandments and a comprehensive body of laws and statutes to Moses. These laws cover various aspects of religious, social, and ethical life, forming the bedrock of Israelite society. The book also details the construction of the Tabernacle, a portable sanctuary designed to house the divine presence among the Israelites, and the establishment of the priesthood.

Leviticus (Hebrew Name: Vayikra)

Leviticus, meaning "and He called," is primarily a book of laws, rituals, and priestly instructions. It focuses on the establishment of a holy community and the means by which the Israelites can maintain their covenantal relationship with God. The book outlines various types of sacrifices and offerings, detailing their procedures and purposes, such as atonement for sin, thanksgiving, and communal worship.

A significant portion of Leviticus is dedicated to the laws of purity and impurity, which govern aspects of daily life, including dietary restrictions (kashrut), ritual cleanliness, and sexual morality. These laws are designed to distinguish the Israelites from other nations and to foster a sense of holiness and separation. The book also includes instructions for the priesthood, outlining their duties and responsibilities in mediating between God and the people. The concept of holiness, both for individuals and the community, is a central and recurring theme throughout Leviticus.

Numbers (Hebrew Name: Bamidbar)

Numbers, meaning "in the wilderness," chronicles the Israelites' forty-year sojourn in the wilderness after their departure from Mount Sinai. The book begins with a census of the Israelite tribes, highlighting their organization and military readiness. It recounts their numerous journeys, encampments, and challenges encountered during their desert wanderings, including episodes of rebellion, murmuring against God and Moses, and divine punishment.

Key narratives in Numbers include the story of the twelve spies sent to scout the land of Canaan, their discouraging report, and the subsequent divine decree that the generation that left Egypt would not enter the promised land. The book also details the rebellion of Korah, Dathan, and Abiram, and the miraculous budding of Aaron's staff, which affirms the legitimacy of the Aaronic priesthood. Despite the challenges and setbacks, Numbers emphasizes God's continued presence and guidance, as well as the preparation of the new generation for entry into the land of Israel.

Deuteronomy **(Hebrew Name: Devarim)**

Deuteronomy, meaning "second law," serves as a recapitulation and expansion of the laws given at Sinai, presented as Moses' farewell speeches to the Israelites on the plains of Moab, just before their entry into the promised land. Moses reviews the history of their journey, reminding the people of God's faithfulness and their covenantal obligations. The book emphasizes the importance of monotheism, the love of God, and obedience to His commandments.

Deuteronomy reiterates many of the laws found in Exodus, Leviticus, and Numbers, often with additional explanations and exhortations. It stresses the consequences of obedience and disobedience, presenting a clear choice between blessing and curse. The book also includes the Shema Yisrael, a central declaration of faith in Judaism, and outlines the principles of justice, social welfare, and the proper conduct of a holy nation. Deuteronomy concludes with Moses' final blessings to the tribes of Israel, his ascent to Mount Nebo, and his death, marking the end of an era and the transition to new leadership under Joshua.

‘Detailed’ Summaries and Events
Book of Genesis

50 Chapters
Covers approximately 2,309 years

Page provided for notes after each book

Why is Genesis so important?

To the original readers of Genesis, the book was valued as a history of their people. It told them the story of how God created the world and dealt with all humanity until He initiated a personal relationship with their forefather Abraham. Genesis revealed to them the eternal promises God made to Abraham, Isaac, and Jacob—promises which extended to their descendants. It provided comfort and hope for the downtrodden Hebrews as they waited to return to their “promised land.”

Genesis offers a thorough background to the rest of the Bible. Here we learn ancient history and geography and are introduced to significant people and events found later in the Bible. God also reveals many facets of His nature through His dealings with people. We learn of the origin of sin, of its destructive effect on humanity. It covers the most time (2,300 years) of all the other books of the entire bible put together. It is overflowing with the beginning of the world and how it developed under God’s plan. It is considered the most important Book of the entire Bible: God’s actual words recorded by Moses at the request of God.

Genesis, the first book of the Bible, tells the story of beginnings: from God's creation of the world and humanity, through the introduction of sin (Adam & Eve, Cain & Abel, Flood, Babel), to the formation of the Israelite nation through patriarchs like Abraham, Isaac, Jacob, and Joseph, establishing covenants and setting the stage for redemption, all while showing human failure and God's persistent faithfulness. Note: The following accounts are drawn exclusively from a combination of authoritative print encyclopedias, published nonfiction books, academic journals, and dictionaries, and my personal knowledge of the Torah.

Main Themes:

- **Creation & Covenant:**

  God creates a good world and establishes special relationships (covenants) with people, especially Abraham.

- **Sin & Redemption:**

  Humanity's rebellion brings sin and death, but God begins a plan to redeem the world through a chosen people.

- **Beginnings:**
  Explains the origin of the world, humanity, marriage, evil, languages, nations, and the chosen family of Israel.

Let us begin our journey through over 2,300 years of history. Sit back, relax and get ready to hear God's words just like Moses did.

Where it all began

Genesis 1-11

The initial chapters of Genesis describe the origins of the cosmos and humanity, setting the stage for the subsequent narratives of the patriarchs.

Creation

Genesis 1:1-2:3

The book opens with the majestic account of creation, often referred to as the "seven-day creation." God, through divine utterance, brings forth the heavens and the earth from a state of formlessness and void. On the first day, light is created, separating it from darkness. The second day sees the creation of the firmament, dividing the waters above from the waters below. On the third day, dry land emerges, and vegetation is brought forth. The fourth day witnesses the creation of the sun, moon, and stars to govern the day and night and to mark seasons. On the fifth day, aquatic creatures and birds are created. The sixth day culminates in the creation of land animals and, most significantly, humanity—male and female—in God's image, granting them dominion over creation. The seventh day is designated as a day of rest and sanctification, establishing the Sabbath. This account emphasizes God's omnipotence and the inherent goodness of creation.

Quick Reference
The Beginning: In the beginning, God creates the heavens and the earth. Initially, the earth is formless and void, with darkness covering the deep.

- **Day 1:** God commands light to exist, separating it from darkness. He names the light "day" and the darkness "night." This establishes the day-night cycle.
- **Day 2:** God creates a "firmament" (often understood as the sky) to divide the waters above and below.
- **Day 3:** God gathers the waters into seas and reveals dry land. He then creates various plants and vegetation on the newly formed land.
- **Day 4:** God creates the sun, moon, and stars to govern day and night and to mark the seasons.
- **Day 5:** God fills the seas with various life forms, including fish and sea creatures, and populates the skies with birds.
- **Day 6:** God creates land animals of all kinds and, as the crowning act of creation, creates humanity in his own image, both male and female. He blesses them and entrusts them with dominion over the earth.
- **Day 7:** God rests from his work of creation. He declares creation "very good" and institutes the Sabbath as a day of rest and remembrance.

God beheld all that He had made and declared it very good. Thus, the seven days of creation were completed, and God rested on the seventh day, making it holy.

The Garden of Eden and the Fall

Genesis 2:4-3:24

Following the seven-day creation, a more detailed account of humanity's origin is provided, focusing on the creation of Adam from the dust of the ground and Eve from Adam's rib. They are placed in the Garden of Eden, a paradisiacal setting, with access to all trees except the Tree of the Knowledge of Good and Evil. God gives a clear command not to eat from this tree, warning of death as a consequence. The serpent, described as craftier than any other wild animal, tempts Eve, questioning God's word and promising god-like knowledge. Eve, and then Adam, partake of the forbidden fruit. This act of disobedience, known as the Fall, introduces sin into the world, leading to a loss of innocence, shame, and a broken relationship with God. Consequences include pain in childbirth for women, toil in labor for men, and ultimately, mortality. Adam and Eve are expelled from the Garden of Eden to prevent them from eating from the Tree of Life and living forever in their fallen state.

Brothers Cain and Abel

Genesis 4:1-16

The first human family outside Eden experiences tragedy. Cain, a tiller of the ground, and Abel, a keeper of sheep, offer sacrifices to God. God accepts Abel's offering but rejects Cain's, leading to Cain's jealousy and anger. Despite a divine warning about sin crouching at his door, Cain murders his brother Abel in the field. God confronts Cain, who denies knowledge of Abel's whereabouts. As punishment, Cain is cursed from the ground and becomes a restless wanderer. God, however, places a mark on Cain to protect him from vengeance.

The Line of Cain and Seth

Genesis 4:17-5:32

The narrative then traces the descendants of Cain, highlighting the development of civilization (city building, music, metalworking) but also the escalation of violence, exemplified by Lamech's boast of vengeance. In contrast, a new lineage begins with the birth of Seth, who is seen as a replacement for Abel. This line is presented as the ancestral line of Noah, emphasizing a connection to God, with the phrase "at that time people began to call on the name of the Lord".

The chapter concludes with a genealogy from Adam to Noah, noting the extraordinary lifespans of these early patriarchs.

Nephilim and the Corruption of Humanity

Genesis 6:1-8

This brief but significant passage describes the "sons of God" taking "daughters of humankind" as wives, resulting in the birth of the Nephilim, described as "heroes of old, men of renown." The exact identity of the "sons of God" is debated, with interpretations ranging from divine beings to human rulers or the Sethite line. Regardless of their identity, this period is characterized by widespread human wickedness and corruption, leading God to grieve over his creation and decide to destroy humanity through a flood.

Noah and the Great Flood

Genesis 6:9-9:29

Amidst the extensive wickedness, Noah is found to be righteous and blameless. God instructs Noah to build an ark, providing detailed specifications, and to gather his family and pairs of all living creatures. The flood comes, covering the entire earth and destroying all life outside the ark. After 150 days, the waters recede, and the ark comes to rest on the mountains of Ararat. Noah sends out a raven and then doves to ascertain the state of the earth. Upon disembarking, Noah builds an altar and offers sacrifices to God. God establishes a covenant with Noah and all living creatures, promising never again to destroy the earth with a flood, and sets the rainbow as a sign of this covenant. God also reiterates the command to be fruitful and multiply and establishes laws regarding the sanctity of life and capital punishment. The narrative concludes with Noah's drunkenness, Ham's disrespectful act, and Noah's subsequent curses upon Canaan (Ham's son) and blessings upon Shem and Japheth.

The Line of Nations

Genesis 10:1-32

This chapter provides a genealogical list of the descendants of Noah's three sons—Shem, Ham, and Japheth—from whom all the nations of the earth are said to have descended. It serves as an ethnological and geographical survey, explaining the origins and distribution of various peoples and languages. This section underscores the unity of humanity's origin while accounting for its diversity.

Tower of Babel

Genesis 11:1-9

The primeval history concludes with the story of the Tower of Babel. Humanity, speaking a single language, settles in the land of Shinar and decides to build a city with a tower that reaches to the heavens, aiming to "make a name for ourselves" and avoid being scattered. God observes their unified ambition and, perceiving it as a challenge to divine authority, confuses their language, making it impossible for them to understand one another. This act leads to the cessation of the building project and the scattering of humanity across the earth, explaining the diversity of languages and the dispersion of peoples.

The Patriarchs

Genesis 11:10-50:26

The second major section of Genesis focuses on the lives of the patriarchs—Abraham, Isaac, and Jacob—and their families, through whom God establishes his covenant and begins to form a chosen people.

From Shem to Abram

Genesis 11:10-32

A genealogy traces the lineage from Shem to Terah, the father of Abram (later Abraham), Nahor, and Haran. The narrative then focuses on Terah's family, who migrate from Ur of the Chaldeans to Haran, where Terah dies. This sets the stage for God's call to Abram.

The Call of Abram and His Journey to Canaan

Genesis 12:1-9

God calls Abram to leave his country, his people, and his father's household and go to a land that God will show him. God promises to make Abram into a great nation, to bless him, to make his name great, and to bless those who bless him and curse those who curse him, and through him, all peoples on earth will be blessed. Abram obeys, taking his wife Sarai and his nephew Lot, and journeys to Canaan. Upon arriving at Shechem, God appears to Abram and promises to give this land to his descendants. Abram builds altars to the Lord.

Abram in Egypt

Genesis 12:10-20

Due to a severe famine in Canaan, Abram and his household go down to Egypt. Fearing that the Egyptians will kill him to take his beautiful wife Sarai, Abram instructs her to say she is his sister. Pharaoh takes Sarai into his household, and Abram is treated well for her sake. However, God afflicts Pharaoh and his household with plagues, revealing Sarai's true identity. Pharaoh rebukes Abram and sends him and his family out of Egypt.

Abram and Lot Separate

Genesis 13:1-18

Upon returning to Canaan, Abram and Lot's herds and flocks become so numerous that the land cannot support them living together. Their herdsmen quarrel. Abram, demonstrating generosity and a desire for peace, suggests they separate, allowing Lot to choose his land first. Lot chooses the fertile plain of the Jordan, near Sodom, while Abram settles in Canaan. After Lot's departure, God reaffirms his promise to Abram, showing him all the land and promising it to his descendants. Abram then moves to Hebron and builds an altar.

Abram Rescues Lot

Genesis 14:1-24

A confederation of eastern kings, led by Kedorlaomer, invades the Jordan Valley, conquering Sodom and Gomorrah and taking Lot captive. When Abram hears of this, he mobilizes his trained men, pursues the kings, defeats them, and rescues Lot and all the captured goods. On his return, Abram is met by Melchizedek, king of Salem and priest of God Most High, who blesses Abram, and Abram gives him a tenth of everything. The king of Sodom offers Abram the recovered goods, but Abram refuses, not wanting to be indebted to the king

God's Covenant with Abram

Genesis 15:1-21

God appears to Abram in a vision, reaffirming his promises. Abram expresses concern about having no heir, and God promises him a son from his own body and descendants as numerous as the stars. Abram believes God, and it is credited to him as righteousness. God then makes a formal covenant with Abram, instructing him to prepare animals for a sacrifice. As the sun sets, a deep sleep falls upon Abram, and God reveals that his descendants will be enslaved in a foreign land for 400 years but will eventually return to possess the land from the Wadi of Egypt to the Euphrates.

Hagar and Ishmael

Genesis 16:1-16

Sarai, unable to conceive, suggests that Abram have a child with her Egyptian maidservant, Hagar, according to the custom of the time. Hagar conceives, and as a result, she despises Sarai. Sarai treats Hagar harshly, causing Hagar to flee into the wilderness. An angel of the Lord appears to Hagar, instructs her to return to Sarai, and promises that her son will be named Ishmael ("God hears") and will be a wild donkey of a man, whose hand will be against everyone and everyone's hand against him. Hagar returns and gives birth to Ishmael.

The Covenant of Circumcision

Genesis 17:1-27

When Abram is ninety-nine years old, God appears to him, reiterates his covenant, and changes Abram's name to Abraham ("father of many nations") and Sarai's name to Sarah ("princess"). God promises that Sarah will bear a son, Isaac, through whom the covenant will be established. God institutes circumcision as the sign of the covenant for all male descendants, to be performed on the eighth day after birth. Abraham and all the males in his household are circumcised.

Divine Visitors and the Destruction of Sodom and Gomorrah

Genesis 18:1-19:38

Abraham is visited by three men, whom he hospitably entertains. They reveal that Sarah will have a son within a year, causing Sarah to laugh in disbelief. The visitors then reveal their intention to investigate the outcry against Sodom and Gomorrah. Abraham intercedes, pleading with God to spare the cities if a certain number of righteous people can be found, progressively lowering the number from fifty to ten. Two angels (two of the three visitors) then go to Sodom, where Lot offers them hospitality.

The men of Sodom demand that Lot bring out his guests for sexual abuse. Lot offers his daughters instead, but the mob persists. The angels strike the men with blindness and urge Lot and his family to flee the city before its destruction. Lot, his wife, and two daughters escape, but Lot's wife looks back and is turned into a pillar of salt. Sodom and Gomorrah are destroyed by fire and sulfur. Lot and his daughters take refuge in a cave, and fearing they will have no descendants, the daughters get their father drunk and conceive children by him, giving rise to the Moabites and Ammonites.

Abraham and Abimelech

Genesis 20:1-18

Abraham moves to Gerar, and again, out of fear, he tells Abimelech, the king, that Sarah is his sister. Abimelech takes Sarah. God appears to Abimelech in a dream, warning him that he will die because he has taken a married woman. Abimelech protests his innocence, and God reveals Abraham's deception. Abimelech confronts Abraham, who explains his fear. Abimelech returns Sarah, gives Abraham gifts, and allows him to settle in his land. Abraham prays for Abimelech's household, and God heals them.

The Birth of Isaac and the Expulsion of Hagar and Ishmael

Genesis 21:1-21

Sarah gives birth to Isaac ("he laughs") as God had promised. Abraham circumcises Isaac on the eighth day. At Isaac's weaning feast, Sarah sees Ishmael mocking Isaac and demands that Abraham send Hagar and Ishmael away. Abraham is distressed, but God tells him to listen to Sarah, promising to make a nation of Ishmael as well.

Abraham sends Hagar and Ishmael into the wilderness of Beersheba. When their water runs out, Hagar despairs, but an angel of God appears, shows her a well, and promises that Ishmael will become a great nation. Ishmael grows up in the wilderness of Paran and becomes an archer.

Isaac as a Sacrifice

Genesis 22:1-19

God tests Abraham by commanding him to sacrifice his beloved son, Isaac, on Mount Moriah. Abraham, in an act of profound obedience and faith, prepares to carry out the command. As he is about to slay Isaac, an angel of the Lord calls out from heaven, stopping him. A ram is provided as a substitute sacrifice. God reaffirms his covenant with Abraham, promising abundant blessings and descendants as numerous as the stars and sand, because he did not withhold his son.

The Death of Sarah and Abraham's Marriage to Keturah

Genesis 23:1-25:18

Sarah dies at the age of 127. Abraham purchases the cave of Machpelah from Ephron the Hittite as a burial place for Sarah, establishing his first land ownership in Canaan. Abraham then sends his servant to his homeland in Mesopotamia to find a wife for Isaac from his own kin. The servant, guided by God, meets Rebekah at a well and recognizes her as the chosen bride. Rebekah agrees to return with the servant and marries Isaac. Abraham later marries Keturah and has several more children, but he gives all his possessions to Isaac, sending his other sons away with gifts. Abraham dies at the age of 175 and is buried with Sarah in the cave of Machpelah. The chapter also briefly lists the descendants of Ishmael.

Isaac and Rebekah

Genesis 25:19-26:35

Rebekah is barren for twenty years, and Isaac prays for her. She conceives twins, and God reveals that two nations are in her womb, and the older will serve the younger. Esau is born first, red and hairy, and becomes a skillful hunter. Jacob is born grasping Esau's heel and is a quiet man, dwelling in tents. Esau despises his birthright, selling it to Jacob for a bowl of lentil stew. Isaac, like his father, goes to Gerar during a famine and tells Abimelech that Rebekah is his sister, but his deception is discovered. God blesses Isaac, and he becomes very wealthy, causing envy among the Philistines. Isaac makes a covenant with Abimelech. Esau marries two Hittite women, causing grief to Isaac and Rebekah.

Jacob Deceives Isaac and Flees to Laban

Genesis 27:1-28:9

As Isaac grows old and blind, he intends to give Esau his patriarchal blessing. Rebekah, who favors Jacob, overhears this and devises a plan for Jacob to impersonate Esau. Jacob, disguised with animal skins and Esau's clothes, receives the blessing from Isaac, which includes dominion over his brothers and fertile land. Esau returns and discovers the deception, leading to his bitter cry and hatred for Jacob. Rebekah, fearing Esau's wrath, sends Jacob to her brother Laban in Haran to find a wife. Isaac blesses Jacob again and instructs him not to marry a Canaanite woman.

Jacob's Dream at Bethel

Genesis 28:10-22

On his journey to Haran, Jacob stops for the night and dreams of a ladder (or stairway) extending from earth to heaven, with angels ascending and descending on it. God stands above it and reaffirms the covenant promises made to Abraham and Isaac, promising to give the land to Jacob's descendants, to bless him, and to be with him wherever he goes. Jacob awakens, recognizes the holiness of the place, names it Bethel ("house of God"), sets up a pillar, and vows to give a tenth of all he receives to God.

Jacob, Sisters Rachel, and Leah

Genesis 29:1-30:24

Jacob arrives in Haran and meets Rachel, Laban's younger daughter, at a well. He falls in love with her and agrees to work seven years for Laban to marry her. However, Laban deceives Jacob, giving him Leah, his older daughter, instead. Jacob confronts Laban, who explains the custom of marrying the older daughter first. Jacob agrees to work another seven years for Rachel, whom he marries a week after Leah. Jacob loves Rachel more than Leah. Leah, though unloved, bears Jacob four sons: Reuben, Simeon, Levi, and Judah. Rachel remains barren. Both women give their maidservants (Bilhah and Zilpah) to Jacob to bear children on their behalf, a common practice of the time. Bilhah bears Dan and Naphtali. Zilpah bears Gad and Asher. Leah eventually bears Issachar, Zebulun, and a daughter, Dinah. Finally, God remembers Rachel, and she conceives and gives birth to Joseph.

Jacob's Prosperity and Departure from Laban

Genesis 30:25-31:55

After Joseph's birth, Jacob desires to return to his own land. Laban, recognizing that God has blessed him because of Jacob, asks him to stay. Jacob agrees to work for a share of the flock—the speckled, spotted, and dark-colored animals. Through a clever breeding strategy, and with divine assistance, Jacob's flocks multiply greatly, making him very wealthy. Laban's sons become jealous, and Laban's attitude towards Jacob changes. God instructs Jacob to return to the land of his fathers. Jacob secretly departs with his wives, children, and possessions. Laban pursues them, but

God warns Laban in a dream not to harm Jacob. They eventually confront each other, and after a tense exchange, they make a covenant of peace at Mizpah, setting up a pillar as a witness.

Jacob Wrestles with God

Genesis 32:1-32

As Jacob approaches Canaan, he sends messengers ahead to Esau, hoping to appease him. He then divides his camp into two, fearing Esau's attack. Jacob sends gifts ahead to Esau. That night, Jacob is left alone and wrestles with a mysterious man until daybreak. The man touches Jacob's hip socket, dislocating it. Jacob refuses to let go until the man blesses him. The man changes Jacob's name to Israel ("he struggles with God") because he has struggled with God and with humans and has overcome. Jacob names the place Peniel ("face of God") because he saw God face to face and yet his life was spared. Jacob continues his journey with a limp.

Jacob and Esau Reconcile

Genesis 33:1-20

Jacob sees Esau approaching with 400 men and prepares for the worst. He divides his children among Leah, Rachel, and the two maidservants, placing the maidservants and their children in front, then Leah and her children, and Rachel and Joseph last. Jacob bows down seven times as he approaches Esau. Esau, surprisingly, runs to meet Jacob, embraces him, and they weep together. Esau initially refuses Jacob's gifts but eventually accepts them. They part ways peacefully, with Esau returning to Seir and Jacob settling in Succoth and then Shechem, where he buys land and builds an altar.

Rape of Dinah and the Vengeance of Simeon and Levi

Genesis 34:1-31

Dinah, Jacob's daughter, goes out to visit the women of the land and is raped by Shechem, the son of Hamor, the Hivite prince. Shechem falls in love with Dinah and asks his father to arrange a marriage. Hamor and Shechem propose intermarriage between their people and Jacob's family. Jacob's sons, particularly Simeon and Levi, are outraged by the dishonor brought upon their sister. They deceptively agree to the marriage on the condition that all the men of Shechem's city be circumcised. While the men are recovering from circumcision, Simeon and Levi attack the city, kill all the males, plunder the city, and take Dinah back. Jacob is distressed by their violent act, fearing retaliation from the surrounding inhabitants.

Jacob Returns to Bethel and the Death of Rachel

Genesis 35:1-29

God commands Jacob to return to Bethel. Jacob instructs his household to put away their foreign gods and purify themselves. At Bethel, Jacob builds an altar, and God appears to him again, reaffirming his name change to Israel and the covenant promises. As they journey from Bethel, Rachel gives birth to Benjamin near Ephrath (Bethlehem) but dies in childbirth. Jacob buries her there and sets up a pillar over her grave. Reuben commits incest with Bilhah, Jacob's concubine. Isaac dies at the age of 180 and is buried by his sons Esau and Jacob.

Descendants of Esau

Genesis 36:1-43

This chapter provides a detailed genealogy of Esau and his descendants, who settled in the hill country of Seir and became the Edomites. It lists his wives, sons, grandsons, and the chiefs of Edom, further distinguishing the lineage of Esau from that of Jacob.).

Joseph's Dreams and Jealousy of His Brothers

Genesis 37:1-36

Joseph, Jacob's favorite son, is seventeen years old and tends the flocks with his brothers. Jacob makes him a special coat of many colors, further fueling his brothers' resentment. Joseph has two dreams: in the first, his brothers' sheaves of grain bow down to his; in the second, the sun, moon, and eleven stars bow down to him. He shares these dreams with his family, which increases his brothers' hatred and even causes Jacob to rebuke him. When Joseph goes to check on his brothers in the fields, they conspire to kill him. Reuben intervenes, suggesting they throw him into a pit instead, intending to rescue him later.

However, Judah suggests selling Joseph to a passing caravan of Ishmaelites/Midianites. They sell him for twenty shekels of silver. The brothers then dip Joseph's coat in goat's blood and present it to Jacob, leading him to believe that Joseph has been devoured by a wild animal. Jacob mourns deeply.

Judah and Tamar

Genesis 38:1-30

This chapter is an interlude, focusing on Judah. Judah marries a Canaanite woman and has three sons: Er, Onan, and Shelah. Er marries Tamar but dies without children. Onan is instructed to fulfill the levirate marriage duty but spills his seed on the ground, and God strikes him dead. Judah promises Tamar that Shelah will marry her when he grows up, but he fails to keep his promise.

Tamar, disguised as a prostitute, seduces Judah and becomes pregnant by him, taking his staff and signet as a pledge. When Judah learns of her pregnancy, he orders her to be burned, but she reveals the pledge, proving Judah is the father. Judah acknowledges his paternity, saying, "She is more righteous than I." Tamar gives birth to twins, Perez and Zerah, through whom the Davidic line will eventually come.

Joseph in Potiphar's House

Genesis 39:1-23

Joseph is taken to Egypt and sold to Potiphar, an officer of Pharaoh and captain of the guard. God is with Joseph, and he prospers, becoming Potiphar's trusted overseer. Potiphar's wife attempts to seduce Joseph repeatedly. Joseph resists, citing his loyalty to Potiphar and his fear of God. One day, she grabs his cloak, and he flees, leaving his cloak behind. She falsely accuses him of attempted rape. Potiphar, enraged, has Joseph thrown into prison.

Joseph Interprets Dreams While in Prison

Genesis 40:1-23 In prison, Joseph encounters Pharaoh's chief cupbearer and chief baker, who have both had troubling dreams. Joseph, acknowledging that interpretation belongs to God, interprets their dreams. The cupbearer's dream signifies his restoration to his position in three days, while the baker's dream foretells his execution in three days. Joseph asks the cupbearer to remember him when he is restored, but the cupbearer forgets him.

Pharaoh's Dreams and Joseph's Release

Genesis 41:1-57

Two years later, Pharaoh has two disturbing dreams: seven fat cows are devoured by seven thin cows, and seven full heads of grain are swallowed by seven thin, scorched heads of grain. None of Pharaoh's wise men or magicians can interpret them. The chief cupbearer finally remembers Joseph and tells Pharaoh about his dream-interpreting ability. Joseph is brought from prison and, attributing the ability to God, interprets Pharaoh's dreams as seven years of abundant harvest followed by seven years of severe famine throughout Egypt.

He advises Pharaoh to appoint a wise and discerning man to oversee the collection and storage of grain during the years of plenty. Impressed, Pharaoh appoints Joseph as his second-in-command, giving him his signet ring, fine linen clothes, and a gold chain. Joseph marries Asenath, daughter of Potiphera, priest of On, and has two sons, Manasseh and Ephraim. Joseph oversees the storage of grain, and when the famine strikes, he opens the storehouses and sells grain to the Egyptians and people from surrounding lands.

Joseph's Brothers Come to Egypt

Genesis 42:1-38

When the famine reaches Canaan, Jacob sends his ten older sons to Egypt to buy grain, but he keeps Benjamin with him, fearing harm. The brothers come before Joseph, who recognizes them but they do not recognize him. Joseph accuses them of being spies. He tests them by imprisoning them for three days and then demands that they bring their youngest brother,

Benjamin, to prove their honesty. He keeps Simeon as a hostage and sends the others back with grain, secretly returning their money to their sacks. On their journey home, they discover the money, filling them with fear. Jacob is distraught at the thought of losing Benjamin.

The Brothers Return with Benjamin

Genesis 43:1-34

The famine persists, and the family runs out of grain. Jacob is reluctant to send Benjamin, but Judah pledges his own life for Benjamin's safety. The brothers return to Egypt with Benjamin and double the money to repay what was found in their sacks. Joseph sees Benjamin and is deeply moved. He invites them to eat with him, and they are astonished when they are seated in order of their age. Joseph gives Benjamin five times as much food as the others.

The Silver Cup and Joseph's Revelation

Genesis 44:1-45:28

Joseph orders his steward to fill his brothers' sacks with grain and to place his silver cup in Benjamin's sack. As they depart, Joseph sends his steward to pursue them and accuse them of theft. The cup is found in Benjamin's sack. The brothers are brought back to Joseph, who declares that Benjamin will become his slave. Judah makes a passionate plea, offering himself as a slave in Benjamin's place, recounting Jacob's deep love for Benjamin and the grief that would befall their father. Overcome with emotion, Joseph reveals his identity to his brothers, weeping openly. He reassures them that God sent him ahead to preserve their lives and instructs them to bring their father and all their households to Egypt, promising them the best of the land of Goshen. He sends them back with wagons, provisions, and new clothes, and Benjamin receives special gifts.

Jacob Goes to Egypt

Genesis 46:1-47:31

Jacob and his entire household journey to Egypt. On the way, God speaks to Jacob in a vision at Beersheba, reassuring him not to be afraid to go to Egypt, promising to make him a great nation there and to bring his descendants back to Canaan. The text lists the seventy members of Jacob's household who came to Egypt. Joseph meets his father, and they embrace and weep. Joseph presents his father and some of his brothers to Pharaoh, who grants them the land of Goshen. Joseph manages the famine, collecting all the money, livestock, and eventually the land of the Egyptians in exchange for food, making them servants of Pharaoh. Jacob lives in Egypt for seventeen years, and before his death, he makes Joseph promise to bury him in Canaan with his ancestors.

Jacob’s Surprise Blessing on Ephraim and Manasseh

Genesis 48:1-22

As Jacob's death approaches, Joseph brings his two sons, Manasseh and Ephraim, to him for a blessing. Jacob adopts them as his own sons, placing them on par with Reuben and Simeon. He then crosses his hands, placing his right hand (the hand of the greater blessing) on Ephraim, the younger son, and his left hand on Manasseh, the older. Joseph tries to correct him, but Jacob insists, stating that Ephraim will be greater than Manasseh. Jacob blesses them, invoking the God of Abraham and Isaac, and promises them a double portion of the inheritance.

Jacob's Prophetic Blessings on His Sons

Genesis 49:1-28

Jacob gathers all his sons and delivers prophetic blessings (and curses) to each of them, foretelling their future and the destiny of their tribes.

- **Reuben:** Loses his birthright due to his defilement of his father's bed.
- **Simeon and Levi:** Cursed for their violent anger in the Dinah incident, destined to be scattered in Israel.
- **Judah:** Receives the royal blessing, with the scepter not departing from Judah until Shiloh (a messianic figure) comes.
- **Zebulun:** Will dwell by the sea.
- **Issachar:** A strong donkey, bowing down to burdens.
- **Dan:** A serpent by the path, a viper by the road.
- **Gad:** Attacked by raiders but will raid at their heels.
- **Asher:** His food will be rich.
- **Naphtali:** A doe set free.
- **Joseph:** A fruitful vine, blessed with strength and prosperity, receiving blessings from heaven and earth.
- **Benjamin:** A ravenous wolf. Jacob concludes by instructing his sons to bury him in the cave of Machpelah.

Deaths of Jacob and Joseph

Genesis 49:29-50:26

Jacob dies and is embalmed, a practice learned from the Egyptians. Joseph and his brothers, along with a large retinue, carry Jacob's body to Canaan and bury him in the cave of Machpelah, as he requested. After their father's death, Joseph's brothers fear that he will now take revenge on them. They send a message to Joseph, reminding him of their father's dying wish for reconciliation. Joseph reassures them, stating, "You intended to harm me, but God intended it for good to accomplish what is now being done, the saving of many lives." He promises to provide for them and their families. Joseph lives to see his great-grandchildren. Before his death at 110 years old, he makes his brothers promise to carry his bones out of Egypt when God leads them back to the Promised Land. Joseph is embalmed and placed in a coffin in Egypt, awaiting the Exodus.

> ***The Book of Genesis thus concludes with the Israelite family established in Egypt, setting the stage for the subsequent narrative of their enslavement and eventual liberation in the Book of Exodus.***

Genesis Notes

'Detailed' Summaries and Events

Book of Exodus

40 Chapters
Covers approximately 80 years

Page provided for notes after each book

The Book of Exodus details the enslavement of Israelites in Egypt, God's calling of Moses to lead them out, the Ten Plagues on Egypt culminating in the Passover, the miraculous parting of the Red Sea for their escape, and their journey to Mount Sinai, where God establishes a covenant with them, gives the Ten Commandments and laws, and provides blueprints for the Tabernacle, all while depicting Israel's struggles with faith and rebellion, like the golden calf incident, establishing them as a nation under God's guidance.
Key Sections:

Major Themes:

- Redemption & Freedom: God's power to liberate His people from slavery.
- Covenant: God's special relationship and legal agreement with Israel.
- God's Presence: The desire for God to dwell among His people (Tabernacle).
- Faith vs. Rebellion: Israel's consistent struggle to trust God, highlighted by the golden calf.

Chapter 1 Exodus

Israelites in Bondage

In this opening chapter. The scene is set with the Israelites in Egypt, who have multiplied exceeding. The new Pharaoh, who didn't know Joseph, sees them as a threat. To counter this perceived threat, Pharaoh orders harsh labor and affliction upon the Israelites. He also orders the midwives to kill any newborn Hebrew boy, but the midwives fear God and do not obey Pharaoh.

Chapter 2 Exodus

Birth and Early Life of Moses

We are introduced to Moses. His mother hides him to save him from Pharaoh's decree and places him in a basket on the Nile. He is found by Pharaoh's daughter and raised as an Egyptian prince. Later, Moses witnesses an Egyptian beating a Hebrew and kills the Egyptian. When Pharaoh finds out, Moses flees to Midian, where he marries and starts a family.

Chapter 3 Exodus

Moses and the Burning Bush

Moses encounters a burning bush that is not consumed by the flames. It is here that God speaks to him, revealing His name as "I AM" and commissions Moses to deliver the Israelites from Egypt. God assures Moses that He will be with him and gives him a sign that will convince the Israelites that God has sent him.

Chapter 4 Exodus

Signs and Wonders

Despite God's assurance, Moses doubts his ability to convince the Israelites and Pharaoh. In response, God equips Moses with miraculous signs, such as turning his staff into a snake. God instructs Moses to return to Egypt. Along the way, Moses' wife, Zipporah, circumcises their son to avert God's wrath.

Chapter 5 Exodus

Pharaoh's Hardened Heart

Moses and Aaron ask Pharaoh to let the Israelites go to worship God. Pharaoh not only refuses but also increases the Israelites' workload, making their lives even more miserable.

The Israelites blame Moses and Aaron for their increased suffering, and Moses questions why God has allowed this to happen.

Chapter 6 Exodus

God's Covenant Renewed

God speaks to Moses again, reassuring him that He will deliver the Israelites. He establishes His covenant with them, promising to bring them into the Promised Land.

This chapter also includes the genealogy of Moses and Aaron, establishing their lineage and authority.

Chapter 7 Exodus

The First Plague – Water Turns to Blood

God gives Moses and Aaron the task of showing His signs and wonders in Egypt. Aaron's staff turns into a snake before Pharaoh, but Pharaoh's magicians replicate the miracle, hardening Pharaoh's heart.

The 1st plague strikes as Aaron turns the Nile River into blood. The fish die, and the river stinks, but Pharaoh remains unmoved.

Chapter 8 Exodus

2nd, 3rd & 4th Plagues: Frogs, Gnats, and Flies

God sends a plague (2nd) of frogs upon Egypt. Pharaoh promises to let the Israelites go if Moses removes the frogs, but once they are gone, Pharaoh hardens his heart.

Next (3rd), God turns the dust into gnats that infest Egypt. Then, God sends (4th) a swarm of flies, which leads Pharaoh to negotiate with Moses, but again he goes back on his word.

Chapter 9 Exodus

5th, 6th & 7th Plagues: Livestock, Boils, and Hail

God continues to send plagues. The 5th plague causes the Egyptian livestock to die. Then (6th), boils break out on the people and animals. The 7th plague is hail, which destroys crops and livestock. Pharaoh admits his sin but, once again, hardens his heart when the plague is lifted.

Chapter 10 Exodus

8th & 9th Plagues: Locusts and Darkness

God sends a plague of locusts that devour what was left after the hail. Pharaoh admits his sin and asks for forgiveness but changes his mind after the plague is lifted.

Then, a deep darkness covers Egypt for three days. Pharaoh tries to negotiate terms with Moses but then threatens him with death if he sees him again.

Chapter 11 Exodus

10th and Final Plague

God tells Moses about the last plague, where every firstborn in Egypt will die. God also makes the Israelites find favor in the sight of Egyptians, who give them gold and silver.
Moses announces the final plague to Pharaoh, who still doesn't listen. Moses leaves Pharaoh's presence in anger.

Chapter 12 Exodus

The Passover

God instructs the Israelites on how to observe the Passover. They are to slaughter a lamb and mark their doorposts with its blood, which will protect them from the final plague.

Pharaoh finally relents after the death of the firstborns and urges the Israelites to leave Egypt. They leave in haste, with unleavened bread.

Chapter 13 Exodus

The Feast of Unleavened Bread

God commands the Israelites to consecrate all firstborn and to observe the Feast of Unleavened Bread annually. They must also tell their children about the Exodus.
God guides the Israelites with a pillar of cloud by day and a pillar of fire by night, leading them away from the Philistines and towards the Red Sea.
(The Great Journey begins)

Chapter 14 Exodus

Red Sea Crossing

Pharaoh pursues the Israelites with his army. The Israelites are terrified, but Moses reassures them that God will fight for them.

God parts the Red Sea, and the Israelites cross on dry ground. When the Egyptians follow, the waters return and drown them.

Chapter 15 Exodus

The Song of Moses

The Israelites sing a song of triumph, praising God for delivering them. Miriam, Moses' sister, leads the women in dancing and singing.

The people grumble when they find the water at Marah bitter. God shows Moses a tree that makes the water sweet.

Chapter 16 Exodus

Manna and Quail

As the Israelites continue through the wilderness, they grumble due to hunger. God responds by providing them with manna, a bread-like substance, and quail.
Moses instructs them to gather only what they need for each day, and on the sixth day, they should gather enough for the Sabbath, on which they should not work.

Chapter 17 Exodus

Water from the Rock

The Israelites are again in distress, this time due to a lack of water. They quarrel with Moses, who cries out to God.

God instructs Moses to strike a rock with his staff, from which water flows. Additionally, the Israelites fight against the Amalekites and win with the help of God.

Chapter 18 Exodus

Advice from Jethro

Jethro, Moses' father-in-law, visits Moses and is amazed by what God has done for the Israelites. He offers sacrifices to God.

Seeing that Moses is overwhelmed with settling disputes among the people, Jethro suggests appointing other trustworthy individuals to share the load, leaving only the most difficult cases for Moses.

Chapter 19 Exodus

Arriving at Mount Sinai

The Israelites reach Mount Sinai, where Moses ascends the mountain to speak with God. God tells Moses that if the Israelites keep His covenant, they will be His treasured possession.

Moses conveys God's words to the people, and they agree to do as the Lord commands. They consecrate themselves and, amid thunder and lightning, God descends upon Mount Sinai.

Chapter 20 Exodus

The Ten Commandments

God gives the Ten Commandments to Moses on Mount Sinai. These commandments form the basis of moral living and the Israelites' covenant with God.
The people are afraid when they see the thunder and lightning, and the mountain in smoke. They stand at a distance and ask Moses to speak to God for them.

Ten Commandments list

1. You *shall* have no other gods before me.
2. You *shall* *not* make any idols.
3. You shall *not* take the name of the Lord your God in vain.
4. You shall Keep the Sabbath day holy.
5. You shall Honor your father and your mother.
6. You shall *not* murder.
7. You shall *not* commit adultery.
8. You shall *not* steal.
9. You shall *not* bear false witness against your neighbor.
10. You shall *not* covet.

There are three 'you shall' and seven you 'shall not' commandments.

Chapter 21 Exodus

Laws About Slaves and Personal Injury

God provides more laws through Moses. This chapter contains regulations regarding the treatment of slaves and the consequences of personal injuries.
It includes the famous law of retaliation, "an eye for an eye," outlining justice for injuries.

Chapter 22 Exodus

Property Laws and Social Responsibility

This chapter details laws regarding the protection of property and restitution for theft or damage. It also includes various social responsibilities, such as protecting the rights of the vulnerable.

There are also specific laws against sorcery, bestiality, and idolatry, emphasizing the importance of justice and moral living.

Chapter 23 Exodus

Laws of Justice and Mercy

Chapter 23 continues with additional laws regarding honesty, justice, and sabbatical rest. The chapter emphasizes impartiality in judgment and the importance of helping one's neighbors.

God also commands the Israelites to observe three annual festivals: the Feast of Unleavened Bread, the Feast of Harvest, and the Feast of Ingathering.

Chapter 24 Exodus

God's Covenant Confirmed

Moses brings the laws before the Israelites, and they affirm their commitment to following them. Moses builds an altar and offers sacrifices.

God calls Moses up Mount Sinai to receive the tablets of stone with the Commandments. Moses goes up the mountain, where he remains for forty days and nights.

Chapter 25 Exodus

Instructions for the Tabernacle

God gives Moses detailed instructions for building the tabernacle, a portable sanctuary. This includes the Ark of the Covenant, which would house the tablets of the Ten Commandments.

The chapter outlines materials, dimensions, and designs for the various elements of the tabernacle, highlighting the care and precision needed for this sacred space. Among the materials are gold, silver, and bronze, fine linen, and acacia wood. The Ark is described in great detail, along with the table for the Bread of the Presence, and the golden lampstand. The meticulousness of the instructions reflects the importance of the Tabernacle as the earthly dwelling place of God among His people.

Chapter 26 Exodus

More Instructions for the Tabernacle

God continues to give Moses specific instructions for constructing the tabernacle. In this chapter, the focus is on the structure itself, including the tent, curtains, and veils.

The precise details emphasize the importance of creating a sacred and worthy space for the presence of God among the Israelites.

Chapter 27 Exodus

The Altar and the Courtyard

God provides Moses with instructions for building the altar of burnt offerings, including its dimensions and materials. The altar is to be placed in front of the tabernacle entrance. Additionally, God outlines the requirements for the courtyard surrounding the tabernacle, specifying the materials for the hangings, pillars, and the courtyard gate.

Chapter 28 Exodus

Garments for the Priests

In this chapter, God tells Moses how to make the special garments for Aaron and his sons, who will serve as priests. These garments are to be made of gold, blue, purple, and scarlet yarn, and fine linen.

The high priest's garments include the ephod, breastplate, robe, and turban, each with intricate designs and sacred significance.

Chapter 29 Exodus

Consecration of Priests

God gives Moses instructions for consecrating Aaron and his sons as priests. This involves a series of offerings and rituals that will sanctify them for service.

The chapter emphasizes the seriousness and sacredness of the priests' role, who will mediate between the Israelites and God.

Chapter 30 Exodus

The Altar of Incense and the Laver for Washing

God commands Moses to make an altar for burning incense. The altar is to be placed in front of the curtain that shields the Ark of the Covenant.

Furthermore, God instructs Moses on making a special anointing oil and incense, which are considered holy and are to be used exclusively for the tabernacle. It also describes the construction of the *laver*, a bronze basin for washing, which symbolizes the ongoing need for the priests to maintain their ceremonial purity before serving in the Tabernacle.

Chapter 31 Exodus

Bezalel and Oholiab

God appoints Bezalel and Oholiab as the chief craftsmen for the construction of the tabernacle and its furnishings. He fills them with His Spirit, giving them wisdom and skills.

God also emphasizes the importance of observing the Sabbath as a sign of the covenant between Him and the Israelites.

> The children of Israel (and all mankind) shall keep the sabbath (seventh day), to observe the sabbath **throughout their generations, for a perpetual covenant.** Exodus 31:16

> **Editor's Note to Ponder**
> If God's rules are **only** for the Jews, then **who** is the God of **non-**Jews? If the man called Jesus followed God's rules and said they were **in effect "until** heaven and earth **disappear**, not the smallest letter, not the least stroke of a pen, will **by any means disappear** from the **Law**." The Torah and God's law **apply** to **everyone** if **He** is your God.

Chapter 32 Exodus

The Golden Calf

While Moses is on Mount Sinai, the Israelites make a golden calf and start worshiping it. God tells Moses what they have done and threatens to destroy them, but Moses intercedes on their behalf.

Moses descends the mountain, breaks the tablets of the Ten Commandments, and destroys the golden calf. He then calls for those who are for the Lord, and the Levites rally to him.

Chapter 33 Exodus

The Lord's Presence Promised

After the incident with the golden calf, God tells the Israelites to leave Mount Sinai. Moses pleads with God to not abandon them.
God agrees to go with them, and Moses continues to converse with Him in the "tent of meeting." Moses asks to see God's glory, and God agrees to pass by him.

Chapter 34 Exodus

New Tablets and Covenant

God instructs Moses to make two new stone tablets. Moses goes up Mount Sinai, and God proclaims His name and attributes to him.

Moses worships and asks God to go with the Israelites. God makes a new covenant and gives additional laws. When Moses descends, his face shines from being in God's presence.

Chapter 35 Exodus

Sabbath Regulations and Tabernacle Construction

Moses assembles the people and repeats the Sabbath regulations. He then asks for contributions for constructing the tabernacle.

The Israelites bring materials, and skilled craftsmen, including Bezalel and Oholiab, begin the work. The people's hearts are moved, and they give freely.

Chapter 36 Exodus

Building the Tabernacle

Bezalel, Oholiab, and the craftsmen begin building the tabernacle. The people bring more than enough materials, and Moses tells them to stop.

The craftsmen construct the curtains, frames, and crossbars for the tabernacle, following God's precise instructions given to Moses.

Chapter 37 Exodus

Making the Ark and Furnishings

Bezalel crafts the Ark of the Covenant, the table, the lampstand, and the altar of incense. Each item is made according to the specific instructions God provided.
These sacred objects are made from acacia wood and are overlaid with gold, indicating their holy significance in the tabernacle.

Chapter 38 Exodus

Completing the Altar and Courtyard

Bezalel constructs the altar of burnt offering and the basin for washing. He also makes the courtyard's hangings, pillars, and the entrance curtain.

The chapter ends with an account of the materials used in the tabernacle, which were collected through the offerings of the Israelites.

Chapter 39 Exodus

Making the Priestly Garments

The craftsmen make the priestly garments with great care. These include the ephod, breastplate, and other garments for Aaron, who is to be the high priest.

The clothing is made from gold, blue, purple, scarlet yarn, and finely twisted linen, symbolizing the sacredness of the priestly service.

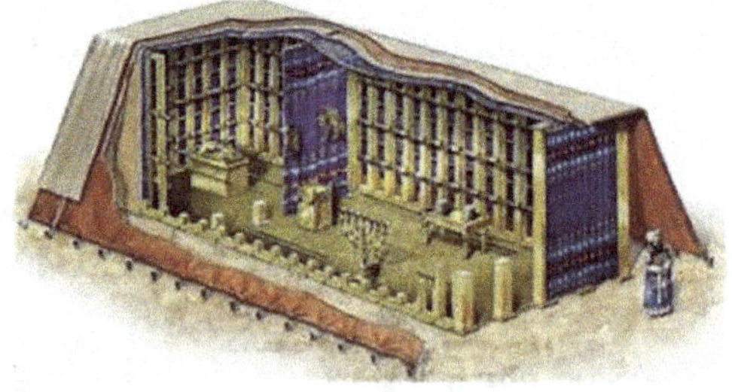

Chapter 40 Exodus

Setting Up the Tabernacle

At God's command, Moses sets up the tabernacle. He places all the objects in their appropriate locations, anoints them with holy oil, and consecrates Aaron and his sons as priests.

Once the tabernacle is set up, the cloud of the Lord covers it, and the glory of the Lord fills it. The cloud will guide the Israelites on their journey.

> ***This chapter concludes the Book of Exodus, showcasing the completion of the tabernacle and the establishment of God's dwelling among His people. The Israelites are now prepared, with God's guidance, to continue their march towards the Promised Land.***

Exodus Notes

'Detailed' Summary and Events

Book of Leviticus

27 Chapters
Covers approximately 1 year

Page provided for notes after each book

Leviticus
Leviticus is the Bible's handbook for holiness, detailing laws for ancient Israel's priests and people on how to live in God's presence, focusing on sacrifices, ritual purity, dietary laws, and moral conduct to maintain a holy, set-apart life {3, 9, 25}. It provides rituals for atonement (sin/guilt offerings), purification (Day of Atonement), and priestly duties, all centered on the theme "You shall be holy, for I the LORD your God am holy" {3, 6, 25}. The book emphasizes that through these practices, a sinful people can approach a holy God in the Tabernacle.

Key Themes & Contents:

- **Sacrifices:** Instructions for burnt, grain, peace, sin, and guilt offerings (Lev 1-7).
- **Priesthood:** The consecration and duties of Aaron and his sons (Lev 8-10).
- **Purity Laws:** Rules on dietary (clean/unclean foods), bodily discharges, childbirth, and skin diseases (Lev 11-15).
- **Day of Atonement:** The central ritual for national purification (Lev 16).
- **Holiness Code:** Laws for holy living in daily life, justice, and sexual conduct (Lev 17-20).
- **Blessings & Curses:** Consequences for obedience or disobedience to the covenant (Lev 26).

Chapter 1 Leviticus

The Burnt Offering

In the first chapter, God calls to Moses from the Tabernacle and begins to give him detailed instructions regarding offerings. The burnt offering is a voluntary act of devotion to God and includes animals such as bulls, sheep, goats, or birds. The person offering the sacrifice must lay their hands on the animal's head, symbolizing the transfer of sin. The animal is then slaughtered, and the priest will sprinkle its blood against the altar.

The burnt offering was wholly consumed by fire, symbolizing complete dedication to God. The offering had to be a male without defect, showing that only the best is to be offered to God. The pleasing aroma of the burnt offering symbolizes God's acceptance of the sacrifice as an atonement for sin.

Chapter 2 Leviticus

The Grain Offering

Chapter 2 of Leviticus focuses on grain offerings, which were also voluntary. This offering is composed of fine flour, olive oil, and frankincense. A portion of it was burned on the altar as a "memorial portion," and the remaining part was given to the priests as food.

The grain offering did not involve shedding blood and was considered a gift offering to God. It symbolized the dedication of the fruit of one's labor to God, and like the burnt offering, it was to be of the highest quality. It was also a recognition that all provisions and blessings are from God.

Chapter 3 Leviticus

The Fellowship Offering

In Chapter 3, we learn about the fellowship offering, which was also known as the peace offering. This offering could be from the herd or flock, and either male or female, but it must be without defect. This offering was unique because it was shared among the altar, the priests, and the person making the offering.

The fellowship offering symbolized peace and fellowship with God. The sharing of the meat between the altar, the priest, and the offeror indicated communion and a state of peace between God and the worshipper. It served as a thankful recognition of God's mercy and provision.

Chapter 4 Leviticus

The Sin Offering

Chapter 4 introduces the sin offering, which was mandatory for sins committed unintentionally. Different offerings were required for different people or groups, such as the high priest, the community, a leader, or a regular person. It involved the laying on of hands and the sprinkling of blood to purify and make atonement.

The sin offering was crucial for maintaining a relationship with God despite human imperfection. It represented the seriousness of sin and the need for atonement. Blood was central in this offering as it symbolized life, and thus, giving life back to God as a form of restitution for sin.

Chapter 5 Leviticus

The Guilt Offering

Leviticus Chapter 5 deals with the guilt offering, which was similar to the sin offering but pertained to unintentional sins that required a repayment. These included sins against holy things or sins against a neighbor. This offering involved an animal sacrifice and often a monetary repayment.

The guilt offering highlighted the idea of restitution in addition to atonement. It was not only about seeking forgiveness but also about making amends for the wrong done. This reflects the principle of restoration and responsibility in one's relationship with God and with fellow human beings.

Chapter 6 Leviticus

Additional Laws for Offerings

This Chapter revisits and expands on the offerings discussed in the earlier chapters. It details additional instructions for burnt offerings, grain offerings, sin offerings, and guilt offerings. The chapter emphasizes the importance of following the prescribed rituals and the responsibilities of the priests in these offerings.

The chapter accentuates the perpetual nature of some offerings, like the burnt offering, which was to be kept burning at all times. For the priests, it outlines their share in the offerings and how they are to be consumed. This highlights the consecrated status of the priests and their critical role in mediating between the people and God.

Chapter 7 Leviticus

More on Sacrificial Offerings

Chapter 7 continues from Chapter 6 and provides more details on the sacrificial offerings, particularly the guilt and fellowship offerings. It outlines the portions that belong to the priests and what should be consumed by the offeror. It also reiterates the prohibition of eating fat and blood.

The emphasis on not consuming blood resonates with the notion that life belongs to God. This chapter further underlines the significance of offerings as acts of worship and the importance of adherence to God's commandments in expressing devotion and maintaining communion with Him.

Chapter 8 Leviticus

The Ordination of Aaron and His Sons

Focus shifts to the priesthood, with a detailed account of the ordination of Aaron and his sons. Moses follows God's instructions in anointing them with oil and blood, and dressing them in holy garments. They also offer sacrifices as part of the ordination process.

The ordination of Aaron and his sons symbolizes their consecration and dedication to serving God on behalf of the people. The rituals, garments, and anointing emphasize the gravity and sacredness of their duties as priests.

Chapter 9 Leviticus

Aaron's First Offerings

Chapter 9 narrates Aaron's first acts as a priest. He performs burnt offerings and sin offerings for himself and the people. The chapter culminates with the glory of the Lord appearing to all the people, and fire coming out from His presence to consume the offerings on the altar.

This chapter marks the commencement of the priestly ministry of Aaron and his sons. The appearance of the Lord's glory and the divine fire consuming the offerings signify God's approval and acceptance of the priesthood and the offerings. It's a powerful affirmation of the establishment of the priestly service.

Chapter 10 Leviticus

The Death of Aaron's sons, Nadab and Abihu

In Chapter 10, tragedy strikes as Aaron's sons, Nadab and Abihu, offer unauthorized fire before the Lord. This results in divine fire consuming them. Aaron and his remaining sons are commanded not to mourn but to continue their priestly duties. The chapter also includes additional instructions regarding the consumption of holy offerings.

The deaths of Nadab and Abihu serve as a stark reminder of the sacredness of approaching God and the seriousness with which His commandments must be taken. Their deaths underscore the weightiness of the priestly role and the absolute respect for God's holiness.

Chapter 11 Leviticus

Clean and Unclean Animals

Outlines the dietary laws given to the Israelites, specifying clean and unclean animals. God instructs the Israelites on which animals they can eat, and which ones are forbidden, such as certain mammals, birds, fish, and insects. The chapter categorizes animals based on their characteristics, such as whether they chew cud or have split hooves, and lists various creatures considered unclean. These laws are part of maintaining ritual purity and distinguishing the Israelites from other nations. The chapter concludes by stressing the importance of holiness, urging the Israelites to be set apart by following God's commands on what is clean and unclean. The dietary laws were a tool to set Israel apart, and they still offer valuable lessons today about living distinctively as God's people.

The following is a short list of clean and unclean foods. Please refer to Leviticus 11 or Deuteronomy 14 for a complete listing.

Two Animal Classes
God created two basic classes of animals in relation to man's diet. Those that benefit our health are called clean foods and those that do not (they are a detriment to our health and wellbeing) are labeled in the Bible as unclean. We find this critical information regarding which meats are good for us (clean) and which are not (unclean) in Leviticus 11 and Deuteronomy 14.

> NOTE: God created all of these. He knows which are good for us and which are not. If He says don't eat them, then trust Him, not you.

In spite of what many believers think, the Bible does not, in the Old or New Testaments, abolish or do away with God's laws about foods that he created either to be eaten (clean) or avoided (unclean).

Below is a list of common meats and fishes divided by whether the Bible considers them clean or unclean to eat. Please note that this list does not denote every animal or insect in existence and where it is classified. When in doubt, it is best to consider a meat unfit for human consumption.

Meats that are GOOD to eat

Clean Land Animals
Antelope - Buffalo - Caribou - Cattle (Beef, Veal) - Deer - Elk - Gazelle - Giraffe - Goat - Hart - Ibex - Moose - Ox - Reindeer - Sheep

Clean Birds
Chicken - Dove - Duck - Goose - Pheasant - Pigeon - Prairie chicken - Quail - Sparrow (plus any other songbirds) - Swan - Turkey

Insects
Clean insects include types of locusts that may include crickets and grasshoppers

Clean Fish

Albacore (Crevalle, Horse mackerel - Anchovy - Barracuda - Bass - Bluebill Sunfish - Bluefish - Bluegill - Bowfin - Buffalofish - Carp - Cod - Flounder (Dab, Gray, Lemon Sole, Red, or Yellowfish Grouper, - Gulf - Pike - Haddock - Hake - Halibut - Hardhead - Herring (Alewife, Branch, Glut. Lake, River, Sea Herrings) - Kingfish - Mackerel (Cobia) - Minnow - Mullet - Orange Roughy - Perch (Bream) - Pike (Pickerel, Jack) - Pollack (Pollock, Boston Bluefish) Red Snapper - Redfish - Salmon (Chum, Coho, King, Pink or Red) - Sardine (Pilchard) - Sea Bass - Smelt - Snapper - Spanish Mackerel - Steelhead - Striped Bass - Sunfish - Trout (Gray Sea, Lake, Sand Sea, White Sea, Spotted Sea Trouts, Weakfish) - Tuna - Whitefish - Whiting (Silver Hake) - Winter Flounder, Yellow Tail - Yellow Perch

Meats that are NOT Good to eat

Unclean Land Animals

Armadillo - Ass - Badger - Bear - Beaver - Boar - Camel - Cat - Ch eetah - Coyote - Dog - Donkey - Elephant - Fox - Gorilla - Groundh og - Hare - Hippopotamus - Horse - Hyena - Jackal - Kangaroo - Leopard - Lion - Llama (alpaca, vicuña) - Mole - Monkey - Mouse - Mule - Muskrat - Onager - Opos sum - Panther - Peccary - Pig (hog, bacon, ham, lard, pork) - Porcupine -Rabbit - Raccoon - Rat - Rhinoceros - Skunk - Slug - Snail (escargot) - Squirrel - Tiger - Wallaby - Weasel - Wolf - Wolverine - Worm - Zebra

Unclean Birds

Albatross - Bat - Bittern - Buzzard - Condor - Coot - Cormorant - Cr ane - Crow - Cuckoo - Eagle - Flamingo - Grebe - Grosbeak - Gull - Hawk - Heron - Kite - Lapwing - Loon - Magpie - Osprey - Ostrich - Owl - Parrot - Pelican - Penguin - Plover - Rail - Raven - Roadrunner- Sandpiper - Seagull - Stork - Swallow - Swift - Vulture - Water Hen - Woodpecker

Unclean Insects

All insects except some in the locust family should not be consumed.

Unclean Reptiles and Amphibians
Alligator - Blindworm - Caiman - Crocodile - Frogs - Lizard - Newts - Salamanders - Snakes - Toads - Turtles

Unclean Fish and Marine Animals
Abalone - Bullhead - Catfish - Clam - Crab - Crayfish - Cuttlefish - D olphin - Eel - European
Turbot - Jellyfish - Limpet - Lobsters - Marlin - Mussels -
Octopus - Otter - Oysters - Paddlefish - Porpoise - Prawn - Scallop - Seal - Shark - Shrimp - Squid
(calamari) - Stickleback - Sturgeon - Swordfish - Walrus - Whale

Chapter 11 lays down the dietary laws concerning clean and unclean animals. It lists the specific animals that can be eaten and those that must be avoided. It also details the distinctions between clean and unclean creatures in the water, air, and land. The dietary laws played a significant role in setting the Israelites apart from other nations. By adhering to these laws, they maintained ritual purity and demonstrated their obedience and allegiance to God.

Chapter 12 Leviticus

Purification After Childbirth

The laws concerning purification after childbirth are outlined. After giving birth, a woman is considered ceremonially unclean for a period of time and must eventually offer a sacrifice to be purified.

This chapter demonstrates the importance of rituals in restoring purity. While childbirth is not considered sinful, the blood associated with it is viewed as ritually impure. The purification process signifies the restoration of the woman's relationship with the community and God.

Chapter 13 Leviticus

Laws About Skin Diseases

Chapter 13 deals with the identification and handling of skin diseases, especially leprosy. It details the role of the priest in examining the affected person and declaring them unclean if necessary. The chapter also discusses the signs and symptoms that should be used to determine the status of the disease.

This chapter highlights the importance of maintaining physical and ritual cleanliness within the community. The laws were not only about religious purity but also had practical implications for containing the spread of contagious diseases.

Chapter 14 Leviticus

Cleansing from Infectious Skin Diseases

This chapter outlines the procedures for the cleansing of a person healed from skin diseases. This involves a series of rituals, including offerings and the application of blood and oil by a priest.

The cleansing process serves as a public declaration that the person is healed and is ritually pure to reenter the community. It signifies the restoration and renewal of the person's social and religious life.

Chapter 15 Leviticus

Discharges Causing Uncleanness

In Chapter 15, the focus is on bodily discharges and their impact on ritual purity. The chapter outlines the various discharges that render a person unclean and the procedures for purification.

This chapter again underscores the significance of maintaining purity within the Israelite community. The laws regarding discharges touch on both hygiene and the concept of holiness in everyday life.

Chapter 16 Leviticus

The Day of Atonement

This chapter is central to Leviticus, as it details the Day of Atonement, Yom Kippur. This sacred day involves fasting and the offering of sacrifices for the sins of the entire nation. The high priest plays a crucial role, entering the Holy of Holies to make atonement before God.

The Day of Atonement is the culmination of the sacrificial system, as it addresses the sins of the whole community. It symbolizes the mercy and forgiveness of God and the necessity for collective atonement and humility before Him.

Chapter 17 Leviticus

Eating Blood Forbidden

This chapter reiterates the prohibition against consuming blood. It establishes that sacrifices must only be made at the tabernacle, to prevent the Israelites from making sacrifices to goat idols.

The emphasis on not consuming blood reflects the sacredness of life. The centralization of sacrifices at the tabernacle was intended to maintain the holiness and purity of the sacrificial system.

Note:

The Bible forbids eating blood because *blood is considered the life itself*, making it sacred and set apart for God's purposes, primarily *atonement for sin* through sacrifice, as seen in Leviticus 17:11. This prohibition, given first to Noah (Genesis 9) and reinforced for Israelites, emphasized blood's special status, preventing its devaluation as common food.

Modern Processing: Meat in modern grocery stores is largely bled out during slaughter, and the "red liquid" is myoglobin, not blood. Animals are humanely bled during the slaughter process to ensure the meat is largely free of blood. The bright red liquid often visible in packaged beef, commonly mistaken for blood, is actually a water-based protein called myoglobin [2]. Myoglobin stores oxygen in muscle cells, and its color changes depending on its exposure to oxygen and iron content.

Key Reasons for the Prohibition

Blood = Life: The fundamental reason is that "the life of the flesh is in the blood" (Leviticus 17:11, 14). Consuming blood was seen as consuming life itself, which God designated as sacred.

Atonement: Blood was given to God on the altar for atonement (making amends for sin), symbolizing the preciousness of life and the sacrifice required for redemption.

Sacredness: To keep blood precious and distinct from common food, God prohibited its consumption, ensuring people understood its role in sacrifice, not sustenance.

Chapter 18   Leviticus

Unlawful Sexual Relations

This chapter of Leviticus enumerates various laws governing sexual relationships. It lists specific relationships that are forbidden and considered abominations.

These laws were vital in defining the structure and morality of the Israelite community. They were set to ensure the sanctity of family relationships and the moral conduct of individuals.

Chapter 19   Leviticus

Various Laws

A diverse collection of laws that guide everyday living, including respecting parents, observing the Sabbaths, and not practicing divination. It also includes the famous command to "love your neighbor as yourself."

This chapter is fundamental in outlining how the Israelites were to live as a holy and set-apart community. The laws emphasize justice, compassion, and integrity as reflections of God's character.

Chapter 20   Leviticus

Punishments for Sin

Specifies the penalties for various sins, especially those related to idolatry and sexual immorality. The punishments are severe, reflecting the seriousness with which God views disobedience and rebellion against His commandments.

This chapter serves as a stern warning and establishes a sense of accountability among the Israelites. It underscores the notion that living as God's chosen people comes with the responsibility to uphold His statutes, and failing to do so has dire consequences.

Chapter 21   Leviticus

Rules for Priests

In Chapter 21, the focus shifts back to the priests and their conduct. The chapter outlines specific regulations regarding their behavior, marriages, and physical condition. It emphasizes that priests must be without defect to serve in the priesthood.

The strict rules for priests highlight their unique and sacred role in Israelite society. As mediators between God and the people, it was imperative for them to maintain the highest standards of purity and holiness.

Chapter 22 Leviticus

Acceptable Offerings

Continues with regulations concerning the priests, particularly about the offerings they can accept or eat. The offerings must be without defect, and the priests themselves must be in a state of purity to partake in or handle them.

This chapter reinforces the importance of holiness and purity in offerings and those who administer them. It reflects God's perfection and the principle that only the best is worthy of being offered to Him.

Chapter 23 Leviticus

Feasts of the Lord

Outlines the sacred feasts and festivals that the Israelites are commanded to observe. These include the **Sabbath**, Passover, Feast of Weeks, Feast of Trumpets, Day of Atonement, and Feast of Tabernacles.

These feasts serve several purposes, such as commemorating God's acts of deliverance, celebrating the harvest, and providing opportunities for collective worship. They are central to the Israelite's identity and their relationship with God.

> "And ye shall proclaim on the Sabbath day (Seventh day), that it may be a holy convocation unto you: ye shall do no servile work therein: it shall be **a statute forever** in all your dwellings **throughout your generations**." Leviticus_23:21

> **The Appointed Festivals**
> [1]The LORD said to Moses, [2]"Speak to the Israelites and say to them: 'These are my appointed festivals, the appointed festivals of the LORD, which you are to proclaim as sacred assemblies.

The Sabbath (The Seventh Day) Shabbat

3 "'There are six days when you may work, but the seventh day
(Saturday) is a day of sabbath rest, a day of sacred assembly. You
are not to do any work; wherever you live, it is a sabbath to
the LORD.

The Passover and the Festival of Unleavened Bread (Pesach is Hebrew for Passover)

Note: Are Passover and the Feast of Unleavened Bread the same thing? Although many think they are, they're described as two separate Feasts in the Bible. The Feast of Unleavened Bread follows right after Passover, though the two events overlap.

5 The LORD's Passover begins at twilight on the *fourteenth* day of the
first month. 6 On the *fifteenth* day of that month the LORD's Festival of
Unleavened Bread begins; for seven days you must eat bread made
without yeast. 7 On the first day hold a sacred assembly and do no
regular work. 8 For seven days present a food offering to
the LORD. And on the seventh day hold a sacred assembly and do no
regular work.'"

Offering the First Fruits

9 The LORD said to Moses, 10 "Speak to the Israelites and say to them:
'When you enter the land, I am going to give you and you reap its
harvest, bring to the priest a sheaf of the first grain you harvest. 11 He is
to wave the sheaf before the LORD so it will be accepted on your behalf;
the priest is to wave it on the day after the Sabbath. 12 On the day you
wave the sheaf, you must sacrifice as a burnt offering to the LORD a
lamb a year old without defect, 13 together with its grain offering of two-
tenths of an ephah of the finest flour mixed with olive oil—a food offering

presented to the LORD, a pleasing aroma—and its drink offering of a quarter of a hin of wine (A quarter hin is approximately 0.97 quarts or 0.92 liters). 14 You must not eat any bread, or roasted or new grain, until the very day you bring this offering to your God. This is to be a lasting ordinance for the generations to come, wherever you live.

The Festival of Weeks (Shavuot or First Fruits)
15 "'From the day after the Sabbath, the day you brought the sheaf of the wave offering, count off seven full weeks. 16 Count off *fifty days* up to the day after the seventh Sabbath and then present an offering of new grain to the LORD. 17 From wherever you live, bring two loaves made of two-tenths of an ephah of the finest flour, baked with yeast, as a wave offering of first fruits to the LORD. 18 Present with this bread seven male lambs, each a year old and without defect, one young bull and two rams. They will be a burnt offering to the LORD, together with their grain offerings and drink offerings—a food offering, an aroma pleasing to the LORD. 19 Then sacrifice one male goat for a sin offering and two lambs, each a year old, for a fellowship offering. 20 The priest is to wave the two lambs before the LORD as a wave offering, together with the bread of the firstfruits. They are a sacred offering to the LORD for the priest. 21 On that same day you are to proclaim a sacred assembly and do no regular work. This is to be a lasting ordinance for the generations to come, wherever you live. 22 "'When you reap the harvest of your land, do not reap to the very edges of your field or gather the gleanings of your harvest. Leave them for the poor and for the foreigner residing among you. I am the LORD your God.'"

The Festival of Trumpets (Rosh Ha-shanah)
23 The LORD said to Moses, 24 "Say to the Israelites: 'On the first day of the seventh month you are to have a day of sabbath rest, a sacred assembly commemorated with trumpet blasts. 25 Do no regular work, but present a food offering to the LORD.'"

The Day of Atonement (Yom Kippur)
26 The LORD said to Moses, 27 "The tenth day of this seventh month is the Day of Atonement. Hold a sacred assembly and deny yourselves, and present a food offering to the LORD. 28 Do not do any work on that day, because it is the Day of Atonement, when atonement is made for you before the LORD your God. 29 Those who do not deny themselves on that day must be cut off from their people. 30 I will destroy from among their people anyone who does any work on that day. 31 You shall do no work

at all. This is to be a lasting ordinance for the generations to come,
wherever you live. 32 It is a day of sabbath rest for you, and you must
deny yourselves. From the evening of the ninth day of the month until
the following evening you are to observe your sabbath."

The Festival of Tabernacles/Booths (Sukkot)
33 The LORD said to Moses, 34 "Say to the Israelites: 'On the fifteenth day
of the seventh month the LORD's Festival of Tabernacles begins, and it
lasts for seven days. 35 The first day is a sacred assembly; do no regular
work. 36 For seven days present food offerings to the LORD, and on the
eighth day hold a sacred assembly and present a food offering to
the LORD. It is the closing special assembly; do no regular work.

44 So Moses announced to the Israelites the appointed festivals of
the LORD.

Chapter 24 Leviticus

Olive Oil and Bread Set Before the Lord

Contains instructions about the regular offering of bread and olive oil in the Tabernacle. A section of this chapter also includes a story of a blasphemer who is stoned, and the proclamation of the law of retaliation (an eye for an eye).

The continual offering of bread and olive oil symbolizes sustained fellowship and reliance on God. The latter part of the chapter emphasizes the gravity of blasphemy and the principle of justice in the community.

Chapter 25 Leviticus

The Year of Jubilee

Introduces the concepts of the Sabbath Year and the Year of Jubilee. During these times, the land was to be given rest, slaves were to be freed, and property returned to its original owners.

The Sabbath Year and the Year of Jubilee reflect themes of rest, liberation, and restoration. They represent a periodic renewal of the social order and a reminder of God's provision and justice.

Chapter 26 Leviticus

Blessings and Curses

Sets forth the blessings that will follow if the Israelites obey God's commands, and the curses that will befall them if they disobey. The blessings are abundant, while the curses are severe and far-reaching.

This chapter serves to motivate the Israelites to follow God's laws by outlining the direct consequences of their actions. It reflects God's justice and His desire for His people to choose obedience and blessing.

> **Additional Blessings of Obedience**
> "[1]You must not make idols for yourselves or set up a carved image or sacred pillar; you must not place a sculpted stone in your land to bow down to it. For I am the LORD your God. [2]You must keep My Sabbaths and have reverence for My sanctuary. I am the LORD.
> Leviticus 26:1-2

Chapter 27 Leviticus

Laws on Vows

The final chapter deals with the laws regarding vows, specifically vows that assign monetary value to people, animals, houses, and land dedicated to the Lord.

This chapter highlights the gravity of making vows to God. It establishes that when a person makes a vow, they are bound to it, and it must be fulfilled. This underscores the importance of integrity and devotion in one's relationship with God.

> ***This ends the summary of the Book of Leviticus. Leviticus, serves as a manual for the Israelites' worship and community life, centering on the holiness of God and the call for His people to emulate this holiness. It meticulously outlines sacrificial offerings, dietary laws, rituals for purification, moral and ethical conduct, and the sacred feasts, thereby providing a comprehensive guide for the Israelites in both their religious practices and everyday living. Through its detailed regulations, Leviticus emphasizes the significance of purity, atonement, reverence, and moral integrity in nurturing a profound and devoted relationship with God.***

Leviticus Notes

‘Detailed’ Summary and Events
Book of Numbers

36 Chapters
Covers approximately 39 years

Page provided for notes after each book

The Book of Numbers in the Bible chronicles the Israelites' 40-year wilderness journey after Egypt, detailing census counts, laws, and their progression from Sinai to the Plains of Moab, highlighting themes of obedience vs. rebellion, and God's faithful provision despite human failure, as the older, disobedient generation dies off, making way for a new one to inherit the Promised Land. It's a theological narrative about God's faithfulness and the consequences of mistrust, culminating in the new generation preparing to cross into Canaan.

Key Aspects of Numbers:

- **Journey & Stages**:
  Follows Israel's stages: Sinai -> Wilderness of Paran -> Plains of Moab.
- **Censuses**:
  Begins with numbering the people, giving the book its name and showing Israel's growth.
- **Rebellion & Consequences**:
  The people grumble, doubt God's provision, and refuse to enter the Promised Land after spies' negative reports, leading to the 40-year wandering.
- **Faith vs. Doubt**:
  Contrasts the faithless first generation (except Caleb & Joshua) with the faithful new generation.
- **God's Holiness**:
  Reinforces God's presence (Tabernacle) and demands for holiness, with consequences for disobedience.

- **Hope for the Future**:
  Ends with the new generation ready to conquer and settle Canaan, fulfilling God's promises.

Chapter 1 Numbers

The Census of Israel's Troops

God spoke to Moses on Mount Sinai, instructing him to take a census of the entire Israelite community by their clans and families. This census was to include every male over the age of twenty who was able to serve in the Israelite army. Twelve leaders, one from each tribe, assisted Moses and Aaron in this sacred task. The numbers reveal that Judah was the largest tribe, and the total count of men eligible for military service was 603,550.

However, the Levites were not included in this general census. God designated the Levites to be responsible for the Tabernacle of the Covenant, and thus, they were to have a special status among the tribes. The census was not merely an administrative task; it was an act of organizing a people, freshly out of bondage, into a structured community under God's guidance.

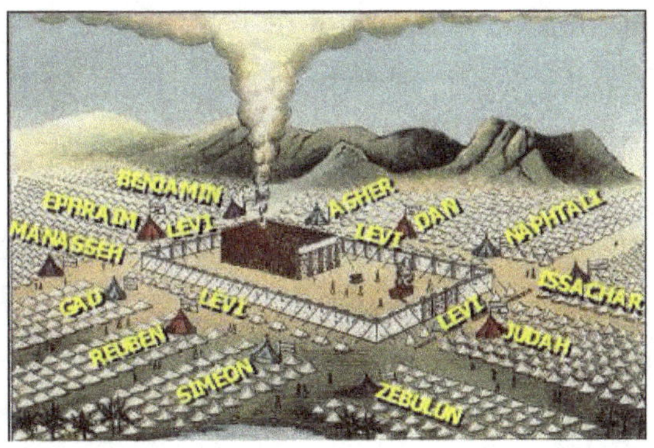

Chapter 2 Numbers

The Arrangement of Israel's Camp

In this chapter, the Lord provides Moses with instructions on how the Israelite camp should be arranged. Each tribe is assigned a specific place around the Tabernacle, with the tribes of Judah, Issachar, and Zebulun to the east; Reuben, Simeon, and Gad to the south; Ephraim, Manasseh, and Benjamin to the west; and Dan, Asher, and Naphtali to the north.

The Levites, however, were to encamp directly around the Tabernacle to guard it and perform their sacred duties. This arrangement was also mirrored in the marching order when the Israelites traveled. The layout of the camp exemplifies God's divine order and the centrality of His presence among His people.

Chapter 3 Numbers

Levites to Serve the Tabernacle

Proclaims the Lord's command to Moses to register the Levites. Unlike other tribes, the Levites were chosen for a sacred task – to take care of the Tabernacle. God claims the firstborn of both people and animals as His own, but here He substitutes the Levites for the firstborn sons of Israel.

> *"Bring the tribe of Levi and present them to Aaron the priest to assist him. They are to perform duties for him and for the whole community at the tent of meeting by doing the work of the tabernacle."* Numbers 3:6-7
>
> *"Appoint Aaron and his sons to serve as priests; anyone else who approaches the sanctuary is to be put to death."* Numbers 3:10
>
> *"The names of the sons of Aaron were Nadab the firstborn and Abihu, Eleazar and Ithamar."* Numbers 3:2
>
> The chapter also mentions a census of the Levites, and unlike the previous census, it includes every male Levite over one month of age. The Levite clans are assigned different responsibilities regarding the Tabernacle, with the descendants of Aaron given priestly duties.

Chapter 4 Numbers

The Duties of the Levites

Here, the Word of God sheds light on the specific responsibilities bestowed upon the Levite clans. The Kohathites are entrusted with the most holy objects in the Tabernacle. Under the supervision of Aaron and his sons, they are to carry the Ark of the Covenant, the table, lampstands, altars, and other sacred articles.

The Gershonites are tasked with carrying the curtains and other fabrics of the sanctuary, while the Merarites are responsible for transporting the frames, crossbars, posts, and bases. These assignments reflect the respect and reverence with which the holy objects should be handled, and the communal responsibility in sustaining the worship of God.

Chapter 5 Numbers

Purity in the Camp

Maintaining the purity and sanctity of the camp. The Israelites are instructed to send away anyone with a skin disease or a discharge, or anyone who is ceremonially unclean due to contact with a dead body. This ensures the holiness of the camp where God's presence dwells. Moreover, the chapter guides us through the laws of restitution. If someone wrongs another, they are to confess the sin, fully reimburse the victim, and bring an offering to the Lord.

The latter part of the chapter presents the trial of the suspected adulteress, also known as the test of bitter waters. If a man suspects his wife of being unfaithful, she undergoes a ritual to prove her innocence or guilt. This reflects the gravity of marital fidelity and the necessity for purity within the community.

Chapter 6 Numbers

The Nazirite Vow

We witness the regulations concerning the Nazirite vow, a voluntary pledge to dedicate oneself to God for a certain period. Nazirites refrain from wine and other fermented drinks, avoid contact with the dead, and do not cut their hair. These restrictions symbolize their wholehearted devotion and separation unto God.

> *23 "Tell Aaron and his sons, 'This is how you are to bless the*
> *Israelites. Say to them: 24 "The LORD bless you and keep you;*
> *25 the LORD make his face shine on you and be gracious to you;*
> *26 the LORD turn his face toward you and give you peace."* Numbers 6:23-26
>
> *Referred to as the Aaronic Blessing or the Priestly Blessing*

Toward the end of this chapter, we find the Priestly Blessing. This is a timeless and treasured blessing that Aaron and his descendants were to pronounce over the Israelites, invoking God's protection, grace, and peace. It's a reminder of the special relationship between God and His people.

Chapter 7 Numbers

Offerings at the Tabernacle's Consecration

In the seventh chapter, the tribal leaders bring offerings for the Tabernacle's consecration. Each day, a leader from one of the twelve tribes brings his offering. Although each offering is the same, the chapter meticulously lists them for each leader, emphasizing the importance of each tribe's individual commitment to the Lord.

The offerings include silver and gold, sacrificial animals, and items for the altar. At the end of the chapter, Moses enters the Tent of Meeting to speak with the Lord, who speaks to him from above the atonement cover on the Ark of the Covenant. This indicates the completion of the Tabernacle and the establishment of communication between God and His servant, Moses.

Chapter 8 Numbers

Setting Apart the Levites

This chapter begins with the Lord instructing Moses on the lighting of the lamps in the Tabernacle so that they shine in front of the lampstand. It reflects the light that God brings into the lives of His people. The chapter also delves into the consecration of the Levites. They undergo a ritual of purification and are presented before the Lord as a wave offering.

> *"In this way you are to set the Levites apart from the other Israelites, and the Levites will be mine." Numbers 8:14*

The Levites are set apart to serve in the Tabernacle in place of the firstborn sons of Israel. Their period of active service is established as between the ages of 25 and 50. Through this, we understand the sacredness and the honor of serving God in the Tabernacle.

Chapter 9 Numbers

The Passover and the Cloud

Emphasizes the importance of the Passover. The Israelites are commanded to observe it at the appointed time. However, provisions are made for those who are unclean or on a journey, so they can celebrate it a month later. This exemplifies God's mercy and inclusiveness, ensuring that all have the opportunity to partake in this significant commemoration.

> *"A foreigner residing among you is also to celebrate the LORD's Passover in accordance with its rules and regulations. You must have the same regulations for both the foreigner and the native-born."* Numbers 9:14

> *"Whenever the cloud lifted from above the tent, the Israelites set out; wherever the cloud settled, the Israelites encamped."* Numbers 9:17

The second part of the chapter describes the cloud that covers the Tabernacle. When the cloud lifts, the Israelites set out, and where it settles, they encamp. At night, the cloud looks like fire. This guidance of the cloud signifies God's continual presence and direction in the lives of the Israelites.

Chapter 10 Numbers

The Silver Trumpets and Israel's Departure

In this chapter, the Lord commands Moses to make two silver trumpets. These trumpets are to be used for calling the community together and for signaling the camps to set out. They also serve a role in times of conflict and celebration. The trumpets symbolize communication, unity, and reliance on God's guidance.

> *"When a trumpet blast is sounded, the tribes camping on the east are to set out."* Numbers 10:5

The latter half of Chapter 10 marks a monumental moment as the Israelites leave Mount Sinai. The cloud lifts from the Tabernacle, and they set out in a specific order by tribe, with the Ark of the Covenant going ahead of them. It's an emblematic departure filled with hope and trust in God's providence.

Chapter 11 Numbers

The People Complain

The journey takes a grim turn as the people complain about their hardships. God's anger is kindled, and a fire from the Lord consumes some of the outskirts of the camp. The Israelites, nostalgic for the food in Egypt, lament the manna provided by God. Moses also becomes overwhelmed with the burden of leading such a vast multitude.

> *"The manna was like coriander seed and looked like resin."*
> *Numbers 11:7*

God responds by having Moses gather seventy elders to share in the burden of leadership. God also sends quail for the people, but His anger is unleashed with a severe plague as a consequence of their ingratitude. This chapter teaches the significance of gratitude and the perils of yearning for what was left behind.

Chapter 12 Numbers

Miriam and Aaron Oppose Moses

Miriam and Aaron, siblings of Moses, speak against him because of his Cushite wife. They question whether God has spoken only through Moses. In this chapter, we see God's swift defense of His servant Moses, affirming that His relationship with Moses is unique.

> *"Miriam and Aaron began to talk against Moses because of his Cushite wife, for he had married a Cushite." Numbers 12:1*

> "Now Moses was a very humble man, more humble than anyone else on the face of the earth." Numbers 12:3

God strikes Miriam with leprosy as punishment. Aaron pleads with Moses to not hold their foolish act against them. Moses, in his humbleness, prays for Miriam's healing. She is confined outside the camp for seven days for her transgression. This chapter shows the importance of respect for God's chosen leaders and the humility that should be in the hearts of the faithful.

Chapter 13 Numbers

The Spies Sent to Canaan

God commands Moses to send spies to explore Canaan. A leader from each of the twelve tribes is chosen. They are to see what the land is like, whether the people are strong or weak, and whether the land is good or bad.

> *And they spread among the Israelites a bad report about the land they had explored. They said, "The land we explored devours those living in it. All the people we saw there are of great size."* Numbers 13:32

The spies return after forty days carrying a cluster of grapes so large that it takes two men to carry it. They report that the land is indeed flowing with milk and honey, but the people are powerful and the cities are fortified. The lack of faith from the spies, except Caleb, spreads fear among the Israelites. This chapter reflects on the importance of trust in God's promises, even when facing immense challenges.

Chapter 14 Numbers

The People Rebel

The Israelites are gripped with despair and fear due to the spies' report. They weep and grumble against Moses and Aaron, wishing they had died in Egypt or the wilderness. Caleb and Joshua, two of the spies, tear their clothes in grief and urge the people to trust in God, but the community talks of stoning them.

> *"Not one of them will ever see the land I promised on oath to their ancestors. No one who has treated me with contempt will ever see it."* Numbers 14:23

God's anger is kindled, and He threatens to destroy the people. Moses intercedes, reminding God of His steadfast love. God pardons them but decrees that none of the adults who left Egypt will see the Promised Land, except Caleb and Joshua. They will wander for 40 years. This chapter demonstrates the grave consequences of unbelief and the power of intercessory prayer.

Chapter 15 Numbers

Laws and Offerings

A reminder of God's laws and the offerings that the Israelites are to make. This includes grain offerings, drink offerings, and offerings for unintentional sins. There's also a provision for the community when they unintentionally fail to observe all the Lord's commandments.

Towards the end of the chapter, a man is found gathering wood on the Sabbath. He is put to death as commanded by the Lord. Additionally, the Israelites are told to make tassels on the corners of their garments as a reminder to obey God's commands. This chapter underscores the importance of obedience and constant mindfulness of God's laws.

> *"The same laws and regulations will apply both to you and to the foreigner residing among you." Numbers 15:16*

Chapter 16 Numbers

Korah's Rebellion

Korah, along with Dathan, Abiram, and 250 Israelite leaders, rebel against Moses and Aaron. They accuse them of exalting themselves above the congregation. Moses tells them that God will show who is holy and who He has chosen to approach Him.

God's judgment is severe. The earth opens and swallows Korah, Dathan, Abiram, and their households. Fire consumes the 250 men offering incense. The censers of these men are to be made into a covering for the altar as a warning to others. This chapter exemplifies the peril of opposing God's appointed leadership and the sanctity of service to God.

Chapter 17 Numbers

Aaron's Staff Buds

To end the grumbling against Moses and to confirm His choice of Aaron and the Levites, God commands Moses to take a staff from the leader of each tribe, including Aaron's, and place them in the tent of meeting. The next day, Aaron's staff had budded, blossomed, and produced almonds.

God commands that Aaron's staff be kept in front of the ark as a sign and a warning. The Israelites fear they will perish in the presence of the Lord, but this chapter reaffirms God's choice of Aaron and the Levites and establishes the authority and sanctity of the priesthood.

Chapter 18 Numbers

Duties of Priests and Levites

God assigns the responsibilities of the priests and Levites. Aaron is responsible for the sanctuary and the altar. The Levites are given to Aaron to assist in the duties of the Tent of Meeting. The priests are to bear the responsibility for offenses against the sanctuary and priesthood.

> *The LORD said to Aaron, "You will have no inheritance in their land, nor will you have any share among them; I am your share and your inheritance among the Israelites." Numbers 18:20*

The chapter also outlines the portions of offerings that are for the priests, including the most holy offerings. The Levites receive the tithes but must give a tenth of these tithes as an offering to the Lord. This chapter establishes the reverence, responsibilities, and privileges of those who serve God in the priesthood and the Levitical order.

Chapter 19 Numbers

The Red Heifer

Introduces the ordinance of the Red Heifer, an unblemished cow that has never been under a yoke. It is to be sacrificed and burned outside the camp, and its ashes are used for purification. This ritual cleansing is necessary for anyone who has come into contact with a dead body.

> *"Anything that an unclean person touches becomes unclean, and anyone who touches it becomes unclean till evening."* Numbers 19:22

This chapter emphasizes the importance of purity and holiness among the people of Israel. Contact with death is a reminder of sin's consequences, and the purification process signifies the restoration of relationship with God.

Chapter 20 Numbers

The Waters of Meribah

As the Israelites journey on, they face a lack of water in the Desert of Zin, leading to further grumbling against Moses and Aaron. Moses and Aaron seek God's counsel, and He instructs Moses to speak to the rock to bring forth water. However, Moses, perhaps out of frustration, strikes the rock twice with his staff instead.

> *"Remove Aaron's garments and put them on his son Eleazar, for Aaron will be gathered to his people; he will die there."* Numbers 20:26

Water gushes out, but God tells Moses and Aaron that they will not enter the Promised Land because they did not trust Him enough to honor Him as holy before the Israelites. (This is why neither Moses or Aaron were allowed to go to the promised land) Later, Aaron dies on Mount Hor after a touching ceremony in which his priestly garments are passed on to his son Eleazar. This chapter reflects on the gravity of obedience and the passing of spiritual mantle from one generation to the next.

Chapter 21 Numbers

The Bronze Snake

This chapter begins with the Israelites defeating the Canaanites. However, as the journey becomes difficult, the people once again complain against God and Moses. The Lord sends venomous snakes among them, and many die. When the people confess their sin, God instructs Moses to make a bronze snake and put it on a pole; anyone bitten can look at it and live.

> *"Then the LORD sent venomous snakes among them; they bit the people and many Israelites died."* Numbers 21:6

Furthermore, the Israelites continue their journey and sing a song of victory at the well given by the Lord. This chapter teaches about the power of repentance and the grace of God in providing salvation.

Chapter 22 Numbers

Balaam and the Donkey

Balak, the king of Moab, summons Balaam to curse the Israelites. God initially tells Balaam not to go, but later allows him to go with a warning to speak only what God tells him. As Balaam rides his donkey, the angel of the Lord blocks his way. The donkey sees the angel and turns away, causing Balaam to strike her. The donkey is given the ability to speak and questions Balaam's actions.

> *"When the donkey saw the angel of the LORD standing in the road with a drawn sword in his hand, it turned off the road into a field. Balaam beat it to get it back on the road."* Numbers 22:23

Finally, Balaam's eyes are opened, and he sees the angel. The angel repeats God's instruction to Balaam to say only what God commands. This chapter demonstrates God's sovereignty over the nations and His power to use even the humblest of creatures to fulfill His purposes.

Chapter 23 Numbers

Balaam's First and Second Oracles

Balaam, unable to curse the Israelites, begins to bless them through oracles given by God. In his first oracle, he proclaims that Israel is a blessed nation and cannot be cursed, for God is with them. King Balak is displeased and takes Balaam to a different location, hoping for a different result.

> "Then Balak said to Balaam, "Neither curse them at all nor bless them at all!" Numbers 23:25

Balaam's second oracle magnifies the blessings of Israel even more. He speaks of a nation that is set apart and cannot be counted among the nations due to their blessedness through God's favor. The chapter emphasizes the irrevocable blessing and favor that God bestows upon His people.

> *"God is not a human, that he should lie, not a human being, that he should change his mind. Does he speak and then not act? Does he promise and not fulfill?" Numbers 23:19*

Chapter 24 Numbers

Balaam's Final Oracles

Balaam delivers his third and fourth oracles. In his third oracle, he sees a vision of Israel's splendor and prosperity. He prophesies that a ruler will come out of Jacob and establish a powerful kingdom. King Balak, frustrated with Balaam's blessings upon Israel, dismisses him.

Before Balaam leaves, he gives a fourth oracle predicting doom for Moab and other nations, but victory and greatness for Israel. This chapter reaffirms God's unwavering favor towards His chosen people and gives us a glimpse of the messianic prophecies.

Chapter 25 Numbers

The Baal of Peor

Depicts a troubling event where Israelites start to indulge in idolatry and immorality with Moabite women. They worship Baal of Peor, which kindles God's wrath. God commands Moses to put to death those who have yoked themselves to Baal.

A plague breaks out among the Israelites. In a brazen act, an Israelite brings a Midianite woman into the camp. Phinehas, a grandson of Aaron, takes a spear and kills both of them, stopping the plague. Phinehas's zealous action for God's honor is commended, and God establishes a lasting priesthood for him. This chapter warns against the seductions of idolatry and the importance of zealous devotion to God.

Chapter 26 Numbers

The Second Census

As the Israelites near the end of their wanderings, God commands Moses to take a second census of the new generation. This is to prepare for the allocation of the Promised Land among the tribes and families of Israel.

The chapter gives a detailed account of the numbers in each tribe. It also mentions that among the people counted, only Joshua and Caleb were part of the generation that left Egypt. This chapter marks the transition to a new generation poised to inherit God's promises.

Chapter 27 Numbers

The Daughters of Zelophehad and Joshua's Commission

Begins with the case of the daughters of Zelophehad. Their father died without sons, and they request a share of the inheritance. God honors their request, and this establishes a legal precedent for inheritance rights of daughters.

> *So the LORD said to Moses, "Take Joshua son of Nun, a man in whom is the spirit of leadership, and lay your hand on him."* Numbers *27:18*

The latter part of the chapter deals with Moses's succession. Knowing that he will not enter the Promised Land, Moses asks God to appoint a leader for the people. God chooses Joshua, and Moses commissions him before Eleazar the priest and the whole assembly. This chapter reflects on justice, and the importance of godly leadership in guiding the people according to God's will.

Chapter 28 Numbers

Daily Offerings

Outlines the daily offerings that are to be made to the Lord. This includes the regular burnt offerings each morning and evening, which serve as an atonement for sin and a means of maintaining a relationship with God.

Additionally, there are Sabbath offerings that are to be made each week, monthly offerings at the beginning of each month, and specific offerings for Passover and the Festival of Weeks. These offerings symbolize the Israelites' continuous dedication and thankfulness to God's providence and grace.

Chapter 29 Numbers

Offerings at the Festivals

The regulations continue, detailing the offerings required during the seventh month. These include the Feast of Trumpets, the Day of Atonement, and the Feast of Tabernacles. These festivals have deep significance.

The Feast of Trumpets is a call to assembly and preparation for the Day of Atonement, a day of reflection, and repentance. The Feast of Tabernacles is a week-long celebration commemorating God's protection and provision during the wilderness journey. These celebrations remind the Israelites, and us today, of the importance of communal worship, remembrance, and thanksgiving.

Chapter 30 Numbers

Vows

Addresses the making of vows to the Lord, particularly focusing on vows made by women. It states that if a woman makes a vow and her father or husband hears of it and says nothing, the vow stands. However, if her father or husband forbids her on the day he hears it, the vow is not binding.

This chapter emphasizes the seriousness with which vows to God should be made and upheld, as well as the authority and responsibility within the family structure in ancient Israel. It serves as a reminder to consider carefully the promises made to God.

Chapter 31 Numbers

War Against the Midianites

God commands Moses to take vengeance on the Midianites for leading the Israelites into idolatry and immorality (as seen in Chapter 25). The Israelites go to war and are victorious, killing the Midianite kings and even Balaam, who had enticed Israel into sin.

The spoils of war are divided between the soldiers, the rest of the people, and the Levites. God also instructs the purification of the warriors and the spoils. This chapter demonstrates God's justice against those who entice His people into sin and the divine guidance in matters of war and purification.

Chapter 32 Numbers

Reuben and Gad Settle East of the Jordan

The tribes of Reuben and Gad, having large herds of livestock, request to settle in the land east of the Jordan River, which is suitable for grazing. Moses initially reacts strongly, comparing this to the unfaithfulness of the spies who discouraged the Israelites from entering Canaan.

However, they clarify that they will fight alongside the other tribes to conquer Canaan before returning to the east of Jordan. Moses agrees to this, and the tribes of Reuben, Gad, and half of Manasseh are granted this land. This chapter highlights commitment to the collective good and the importance of keeping one's word.

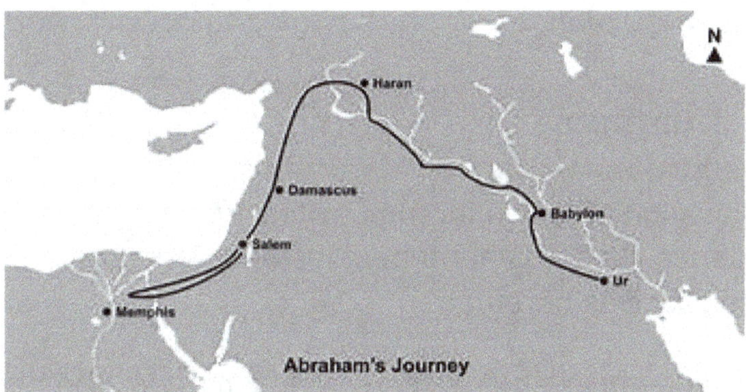

Chapter 33 Numbers

Stages in Israel's Journey

Chapter 33 is a recap of the Israelites' journey from Egypt to the plains of Moab. Through the grace and guidance of God, the Israelites have traveled through the wilderness, and this chapter lists the various places they encamped.

> *"Aaron was a hundred and twenty-three years old when he died on Mount Hor".* Numbers 33:39

Towards the end of the chapter, God commands the Israelites to drive out the inhabitants of Canaan and destroy their idols and places of worship. He also warns them that if they do not do this, those who remain will become a snare to them. This chapter serves as a testimony of God's guidance and a reminder of the importance of obedience in fulfilling God's purposes.

Chapter 34 Numbers

Boundaries of Canaan

God provides specific geographic boundaries for the Promised Land and names the leaders from each tribe who will be responsible for assigning the inheritance.

God's detailed instructions in establishing the boundaries and selecting leaders for the allocation of land shows His sovereignty and wisdom in administrative matters. The chapter reflects God's faithfulness in fulfilling His promises regarding the land that was to be given to the descendants of Abraham, Isaac, and Jacob.

Chapter 35 Numbers

Towns for the Levites

Explains the allocation of towns for the Levites, who do not receive a territorial inheritance like the other tribes. Instead, they are to be given 48 towns, including six cities of refuge.

These cities of refuge are to be places where someone who has accidentally killed another person can flee for safety until a trial can be held. The chapter also outlines laws concerning murder and manslaughter. This highlights

God's concern for justice, protection of the innocent, and the special role of the Levites within the community.

Chapter 36 Numbers

Marriage of Heiresses

The Book of Numbers concludes with the issue of inheritance is revisited, this time concerning the marriage of female heirs. The heads of the tribe of Manasseh express concern that if the daughters of Zelophehad marry men from another tribe, their land will be transferred to that tribe.

God resolves the issue by commanding that female heirs may marry only within their own tribe to ensure that land stays within the tribe. This final chapter closes the book by emphasizing the importance of maintaining tribal heritage and ensuring that the land granted by God to each tribe remains intact.

This ends the summary of the Book of Numbers. As we reach the end of this summary of the Book of Numbers chapter by chapter, we witness how God shepherded His people through trials, triumphs, and tests in the wilderness. Through God's laws, His guidance in war and peace, and His distribution of the land among the tribes, we observe a God who is intimately involved in the lives of His people. The Book of Numbers serves not only as a historical account but also as a spiritual map, guiding us through the complexities of obedience, faith, and God's unyielding promises.

Numbers Notes

'Detailed' Summary and Events

Book of Deuteronomy

34 Chapters
Covers approximately 37 days

Page provided for notes after each book

Deuteronomy is the Bible's fifth book, serving as Moses' farewell address to the new generation of Israelites before they enter the Promised Land, summarizing their history and re-explaining God's covenant, laws (like the Ten Commandments), and instructions for life in Canaan, emphasizing a choice between blessings for obedience and curses for disobedience, all centered on loving and worshipping the one God alone. It's structured around Moses' sermons, reviewing past failures, detailing laws for justice and worship, and calling the people to faithfulness, concluding with his death and Joshua's succession.

Key Themes & Purpose:

- **Covenant Renewal:** A call for the new generation to commit to God's covenant.
- **Obedience & Faithfulness:** Stresses loving God and obeying His laws as the path to blessing.
- **Unique Identity:** Israel's laws set them apart as God's chosen, holy people.
- **Love for God:** A central command to love the Lord with all one's being.
- **Choice:** Presents a clear choice between life (blessings) and death (curses).

Summary of the Book of Deuteronomy Chapter by Chapter

Chapter 1 Deuteronomy

Reviewing the Journey

Moses opens Deuteronomy by recounting the Israelites' journey from Mount Sinai to the plains of Moab, highlighting some of their rebellions and victories. He emphasizes the importance of remembering their history so that the people will obey God's laws as they enter the Promised Land.

Chapter 2 Deuteronomy

Conquering Kings

Moses reminds the people of how they passed through the lands of Esau's descendants and the Moabites after God commanded them not to engage in conflict. He then tells of their victories over King Sihon of the Amorites and King Og of Bashan, and how they took possession of their lands.

Chapter 3 Deuteronomy

Allocating Land

Moses continues his speech by recounting how the lands of Og and Sihon were divided among the tribes of Reuben, Gad, and the half-tribe of Manasseh. He reminds the people that he was not allowed to cross over the Jordan River and encourages them to fully possess the land that God has given them.

Chapter 4 Deuteronomy

A Call to Obedience

Moses urges the Israelites to obey God's laws faithfully and not to add to or subtract from them. He warns against the dangers of idolatry and emphasizes the greatness and uniqueness of God, a stark contrast to the false gods of other nations.

> *"Do not add to what I command you and do not subtract from it but keep the commands of the LORD your God that I give you."*
> Deuteronomy 4:2

Chapter 5 Deuteronomy

The Ten Commandments Revisited

Moses restates the Ten Commandments, the foundational covenant given by God at Mount Sinai. He reminds the people of the awesome circumstances in which the commandments were given and stresses the importance of impressing these laws upon their children.

Chapter 6 Deuteronomy

The Greatest Commandment

Moses expands upon the first commandment with what is commonly known as the Shema: "Hear, O Israel: The Lord our God, the Lord is one. You shall love the Lord your God with all your heart and with all your soul and with all your might." He stresses the importance of teaching these truths diligently to their children and binding the commandments upon themselves as reminders.

> *"Hear, O Israel: The LORD our God, the LORD is one. Love the LORD your God with all your heart and with all your soul and with all your strength. These commandments that I give you today are to be upon your hearts. Impress them on your children. Talk about them when you sit at home and when you walk along the road, when you lie down and when you get up."* Deuteronomy 6:4-7

Chapter 7 Deuteronomy

Conquer and Destroy

Moses commands the Israelites to utterly destroy the nations living in the Promised Land and to avoid making covenants or intermarrying with them. He explains that these nations are a snare that could lead the Israelites away from their true God.

Chapter 8 Deuteronomy

Remember God's Provision

Moses encourages the people to remember how God humbled them and provided for them during their 40 years in the wilderness. He warns that they must not become arrogant or forget the Lord when they enter the prosperous land, attributing their success to their own strength.

Chapter 9 Deuteronomy

Reminders of God's Power

Moses recounts specific events from the Israelites' journey to highlight God's power and faithfulness and their own lack of faith at times. He reminds them of how God delivered them from Egypt through signs and wonders, and how they rebelled against Him despite witnessing His power.

Chapter 10 Deuteronomy

The Second Set of Tablets

Moses narrates how he ascended Mount Sinai again to receive a second set of stone tablets after the first ones were broken because of the golden calf incident. He explains how he remained on the mountain for forty days and forty nights, receiving instructions from God for the people.

Chapter 11 Deuteronomy

Covenant Renewal and Warnings

Moses recounts God's instructions regarding renewing the covenant at Mount Horeb. He warns the people against worshipping other gods, reminding them of the consequences faced by those who disobeyed in the past. He emphasizes the importance of loving and serving God with all their hearts and minds.

> *Therefore thou shalt love the LORD thy God, and keep his charge, and his statutes, and his judgments, and his commandments,* ***forever.*** Deuteronomy 11:1

Chapter 12 Deuteronomy

Centralizing Worship

Moses instructs the Israelites that they must only worship God at the place He chooses, not at the many high places used by the surrounding nations for their idolatrous worship. He emphasizes the importance of offering sacrifices and celebrating festivals only at the designated place, fostering unity and preventing the spread of idolatry.

Chapter 13 Deuteronomy

False Prophets and Idolatry

Moses warns the Israelites about the dangers of false prophets and teachers who may try to lead them astray from worshiping the one true God. He instructs them to test such individuals by their teachings and their results, and to reject those who lead them towards idolatry.

Chapter 14 Deuteronomy

Mourning and the Promise of a New Generation Moses reminds the people of how their lack of faith resulted in them being denied entry into the Promised Land for forty years, with only their children allowed to enter. He tells them to mourn the death of those who will not reach the land and reaffirms God's covenant promise to bring a new generation into the land.

Chapter 15 Deuteronomy

Dietary Laws and Tithes

Moses outlines specific dietary laws regarding clean and unclean animals, reminding the people that these regulations are a way to set them apart and a reminder of their dependence on God for their sustenance. He also establishes regulations for offerings and tithes, ensuring that the needs of the Levites and the poor are met.

Chapter 16 Deuteronomy

Laws for Priests, Levites, and Kings

Moses outlines guidelines for the conduct of priests and Levites, emphasizing their roles and responsibilities in leading the people in worship. He also establishes regulations for the future king of Israel, ensuring that he does not accumulate excessive wealth or engage in practices that would lead the people away from God.

Chapter 17 Deuteronomy

Laws for Judges and Officials

Moses lays out regulations for judges and officials, emphasizing the importance of fairness, justice, and impartiality in their rulings. He warns against bribery and corruption and encourages the people to seek out wise and discerning leaders.

Chapter 18 Deuteronomy

Cities of Refuge and the Avenger of Blood

Moses establishes the concept of cities of refuge, offering protection for unintentional killers who seek sanctuary from the avenger of blood, someone with the right to exact revenge. He also outlines the process for resolving cases involving unintentional killings.

Chapter 19 Deuteronomy

Maintaining Purity and Removing Doubt

Moses provides instructions for dealing with situations that may cause ceremonial uncleanliness, such as contact with death. He also addresses the issue of a doubtful case, where guilt or innocence in a crime is unclear, outlining the process for seeking God's guidance in such situations.

Chapter 20 Deuteronomy

Replacing Leaders and Military Commands

Moses recounts how Aaron, the high priest, dies on Mount Hor and is succeeded by his son, Eleazar. He also outlines various military regulations, including instructions on capturing cities, treating prisoners of war, and dividing spoils of war.

Chapter 21 Deuteronomy

Victories over Kings Sihon and Og

Moses retells the story of the Israelites' victories over Kings Sihon and Og of the Amorites. He emphasizes God's role in granting them victory and warns them against adopting the practices of the conquered nations.

Chapter 22 Deuteronomy

Warnings Against Idolatry and Immorality

Moses delivers a strong warning against the allure and dangers of idolatry, urging the people to remain faithful to the one true God and not to follow the practices of the surrounding nations. He also warns against sexual immorality and outlines specific laws aimed at maintaining purity and honoring the sanctity of marriage.

> *"If you come across a bird's nest in any tree or on the ground, with young ones or eggs and the mother sitting on the young or on the eggs, you shall not take the mother with the young." This phrase refers to a biblical commandment in which teaches compassion by instructing you to release the mother bird if you take her young or eggs, ensuring a long life. It's a lesson in empathy for all creation, training us to feel for others, and is found in Jewish law and interpreted mystically as meditation.* Deuteronomy 22:6 *In modern terms, it also aligns with wildlife protection laws like the Migratory Bird Treaty Act in the US, making it illegal to disturb most wild nests and eggs.*

Chapter 23 Deuteronomy

Qualifications for Leadership and Warfare

Moses establishes specific requirements for individuals seeking leadership positions and participation in warfare. He outlines limitations based on physical characteristics, moral conduct, and past transgressions, emphasizing the importance of maintaining a morally sound and strong military force.

Chapter 24 Deuteronomy

Blessings and Curses

Moses delivers a series of blessings and curses, outlining the potential consequences of obedience and disobedience to God's laws. He foretells a future of both prosperity and hardship, depending on the choices made by us.

> **Note:** Although God gives us the freedom of choice, He did not give us freedom from any consequences of our bad choices (curses). Keep that in mind.

Chapter 25 Deuteronomy

Instructions for Engaging in War and Dividing Spoils

Moses provides specific instructions for engaging in war against enemies and outlines guidelines for dividing spoils of war after victory. He emphasizes the importance of treating women and children with respect and prohibits taking certain items as spoils to prevent the spread of idolatry.

Chapter 26 Deuteronomy

Renewing the Covenant at Moab

Moses gathers the Israelites and leads them in a public renewal of the covenant with God. He reminds them of their history and emphasizes their commitment to follow God's commandments.

Chapter 27 Deuteronomy

Appointing Joshua as Successor

Moses appoints Joshua as his successor and encourages the people to be strong and courageous as they enter the Promised Land. He reassures them of God's presence and encourages them to remain faithful to the covenant.

Chapter 28 Deuteronomy

The Song of Moses

Moses delivers a final song to the Israelites, reminding them of God's faithfulness and their responsibility to obey His commands. He warns them of the consequences of disobedience and encourages them to choose the path of righteousness.

> *All these blessings will come on you and accompany you if you obey the Lord your God." ~ Deuteronomy 28:2*

Chapter 30 Deuteronomy

The Final Counsel and Freedom of Choice

Moses reminds the people of their freedom to choose between life and death, obedience and disobedience to God. He urges them to choose life and to love and obey the Lord their God with all their hearts and minds.

> *"I have set before you life and death, blessing and cursing." God's desire for His people is found in what He recommends: "choose life".*
> Deuteronomy 30:19

Chapter 31 Deuteronomy

Moses' Farewell Address and Song

Moses delivers a final speech to the Israelites, encouraging them to remain faithful to God and warning them against the dangers of idolatry. He also delivers a final song praising God's righteousness and faithfulness.

Chapter 32 Deuteronomy

The Song of Moses

Moses delivers a final song to the Israelites, summarizing the history of their relationship with God and urging them to remain faithful to Him. He warns them against the dangers of disobedience and encourages them to trust in God's love and protection.

Chapter 33 Deuteronomy

Moses' Blessing and Death

Moses blesses each of the twelve tribes of Israel, foretelling their future and their inheritance in the Promised Land. He then ascends Mount Nebo, views the land from afar, and dies at the age of 120. The chapter concludes by emphasizing the leadership of Joshua as the Israelites prepare to enter the land.

Chapter 34 Deuteronomy

Final look and Successor

In the final chapter of Deuteronomy, Moses is unable to enter the Promised Land due to his past disobedience (striking the rock). He ascends Mount Nebo, where God shows him the entire land. Moses dies at the age of 120, and the Israelites mourn him for thirty days. The chapter concludes by emphasizing Joshua's leadership as the Israelites prepare to cross the Jordan River and enter the land God has promised them.

This ends the summary of the Book of Deuteronomy. Deuteronomy underscores the importance of God's Word. It is a vital part of our lives. Although we are no longer under the Old Testament law, we are still responsible to submit to the will of God in our lives. Simple obedience brings blessing, and sin has its own consequences. None of us is "above the law." Even Moses, the leader and prophet chosen by God, was required to obey. The reason that he was not allowed to enter the Promised Land was that he disobeyed the Lord's clear command to speak (not hit the rock with his staff).

Deuteronomy Notes

The Patriarchs & Matriarchs of The Torah

The **Patriarchs**, or *avot* in Hebrew, meaning "fathers," refers to three generations of foundational figures in the Book of Genesis and Jewish tradition: Abraham, Isaac and Jacob.

The **Matriarchs**, or *imahot* in Hebrew, refers to the Torah's four foundational women: Sarah, Rebecca, Rachel and Leah.

Abraham and Sarah were the parents of Isaac who, with Rebecca, parented Jacob. With his two wives Rachel and Leah (and two handmaids, Bilhah and Zilpah), Jacob fathered 12 sons and one daughter, Dinah. The 12 sons would go on to form the 12 Tribes of Israel.

Israel is the name Jacob is given after he wrestles with an angel. Jacob is understood to be the common ancestor from which the Israelites and later, the Jewish people, are descended. This is why Jews are often referred to as *Bnei Yisrael* (the children of Israel) or *Am Yisrael* (the nation of Israel). Abraham and Sarah are still understood as the progenitors of the Jewish people, but other religions and nations also formed from their family tree, while the Jewish people trace their heritage through Jacob.

Judaism, Christianity, and Islam hold that the patriarchs, along with their primary wives, known as the matriarchs (Sarah, Rebekah and Leah), are entombed at the Cave of the Patriarchs, a site held holy by the three religions. Rachel, Jacob's other wife, is said to be buried separately at what is known as Rachel's Tomb, which is about 5.5 miles from the Tomb of the Patriarchs in Hebron, at the site where she is believed to have died in childbirth.

The lifetimes given for the patriarchs in the Masoretic Text of the Book of Genesis are: Adam 930 years,
Seth 912, Enos 905, Kenan 910, Mahalalel 895, Jared 962, Enoch 365 (did not die, but was taken away by
God), Methuselah 969, Lamech 777, Noah 950.
years, Seth 912, Enos 905, Kenan 910, Mahalalel 895, Jared 962, Enoch 36 5 (did not die, but was taken away by
God), Methuselah 969, Lamech 777, Noah 950.

The Beginning (Genesis)

- Abraham**:** The first patriarch, called by God to leave his home for a new land.
- Sarah, Rebekah, Rachel, Leah: Key matriarchs, mothers of the Israelite nation.
- Isaac: Son of Abraham, known for his faith.
- Jacob: Son of Isaac, whose 12 sons became the tribes of Israel; renamed Israel.
- Joseph: Jacob's favorite son, sold into slavery but rose to power in Egypt, saving his family.
- Noah**:** Built the Ark to survive the Great Flood.

The Exodus & Wilderness (Exodus, Leviticus, Numbers, Deuteronomy)

- Moses: The central hero, liberator of the Israelites from Egypt, lawgiver.
- Aaron: Moses' brother, the first High Priest.
- Miriam: Prophetess and sister of Moses and Aaron.
- Joshua: Moses' successor, led Israel into the Promised Land.
- Jethro: Moses' father-in-law, a wise priest who advised Moses.
- Rahab: A Canaanite woman who helped Israelite spies in Jericho.

Old Testament Chapter Summaries

The Entire Old Testament 39 Books
Quick Summaries

Genesis Chapter Summaries
50 Chapters: Genesis chronicles the creation of the world, the origins of humanity, and the beginnings of God's covenant with the patriarchs, Abraham, Isaac, and Jacob. This book lays the groundwork for God's redemptive plan for His people.

Exodus Chapter Summaries
40 Chapters: In Exodus, the Israelites are enslaved in Egypt, but God raises up Moses to miraculously liberate them and lead them toward the Promised Land. God establishes His covenant with Israel at Mount Sinai, giving them His laws and instructions for how they should live.

Leviticus Chapter Summaries
27 Chapters: The chapters of this book delve into the details of the laws and rituals for Israel's worship of God, focusing on holiness, sacrifices, and priestly duties. It emphasizes the need for atonement and purity before a holy God.

Numbers Chapter Summaries
36 Chapters: Numbers records the Israelites' journey through the wilderness, including a census of the tribes, further laws, and their repeated rebellions. It highlights God's faithfulness despite their disobedience and the consequences that come with rebellion.

Deuteronomy Chapter Summaries
34 Chapters: Moses delivers his farewell messages, reiterating the Law and reminding Israel of God's covenant and faithfulness, along with the blessings of obedience and curses of disobedience. This book serves as a reminder and renewal of the covenant before the Israelites enter the Promised Land.

The remaining 34 Books of the Old Testament
Quick Chapter Summaries

Joshua Chapter Summaries
24 Chapters: Joshua, the new leader, leads the Israelites into the Promised Land, conquering the inhabitants and dividing the land among the tribes. The book highlights the importance of obedience to God and His ability to provide victory for His people.

Judges Chapter Summaries
21 Chapters: Judges details the period after Joshua's death, where Israel falls into cyclical patterns of sin, oppression, repentance, and God raising up Judges to deliver them. It reveals the Israelites' ongoing struggle with idolatry and their need for God's constant intervention.

Ruth Chapter Summaries
4 Chapters: This heartwarming story presents a glimmer of hope during the morally-debased time of Judges. Ruth, a Moabite woman, exhibits extraordinary faith and loyalty to her Israelite mother-in-law and exemplifies God's redemption and grace extending beyond borders.

1 Samuel Chapter Summaries
31 Chapters: This book records the transition from Judges to the establishment of the monarchy in Israel, focusing on Samuel the prophet, the rise of Saul as king, and the early reign of David. It explores the complex themes of leadership, power, and obedience to God.

2 Samuel Chapter Summaries
24 Chapters: This continues the narrative of King David's life, covering his

triumphs, his tragic fall into sin, and the consequences that reverberate through his family and kingdom. It shows how God remains faithful even when his leaders fail.

1 Kings Chapter Summaries

22 Chapters: The kingdom of Israel splits into two after the death of Solomon, and this book follows both the northern kingdom of Israel and the southern kingdom of Judah. It details the repeated cycle of idolatry, corrupt leadership, and the voices of prophets calling Israel back to the Lord.

2 Kings Chapter Summaries

25 Chapters: This book continues the history of the two divided kingdoms and their eventual fall into exile, first the northern kingdom of Israel to Assyria and then the southern kingdom of Judah to Babylon. It emphasizes the consistent disobedience of God's people and the consequences that follow.

1 Chronicles Chapter Summaries

29 Chapters: This book revisits the history of Israel through the lens of King David and the genealogy of the nation, emphasizing the Davidic line as central to God's plan of redemption. It focuses on worship and the importance of the Temple.

2 Chronicles Chapter Summaries

36 Chapters: This continues the focus on the Davidic line and recounts the reigns of Judah's kings after Solomon, highlighting the building of the Temple and periods of spiritual revival. It reminds readers of God's faithfulness and His promise of restoration.

Ezra Chapter Summaries

10 Chapters: Ezra records the first wave of Israelite exiles returning from Babylon to Jerusalem to rebuild the Temple. It emphasizes spiritual renewal and the re-establishment of proper worship of God.

Nehemiah Chapter Summaries

13 Chapters: Nehemiah leads the effort to rebuild Jerusalem's walls, facing opposition and focusing on social justice and reviving Israel's commitment to the Law. This book highlights the power of God-given leadership and the importance of perseverance.

Esther Chapter Summaries

10 Chapters: Set during the exile, Esther, a Jewish woman, becomes Queen of Persia and heroically risks her life to save her people from annihilation. This story displays God's providence working behind the scenes even without direct mention of His name.

Job Chapter Summaries

42 Chapters: This poetic book explores the profound mystery of suffering through the story of Job, a righteous man who endures immense personal loss and questions God's justice. Job's unwavering faith and dialogue with his friends ultimately lead to a deeper understanding of God's sovereignty and wisdom.

Psalms Chapter Summaries

150 Chapters: This collection of 150 poems and songs expresses the full range of human emotions – praise, lament, thanksgiving, and cries for help – directed towards God. The Psalms serve as a timeless resource for prayer and reflection on the human experience in relation to God.

Proverbs Chapter Summaries

31 Chapters: This book offers practical wisdom for everyday life, covering topics such as relationships, work, speech, and personal conduct. Written in poetic and memorable sayings, Proverbs aims to guide individuals towards a life of righteousness and success.

Ecclesiastes Chapter Summaries

12 Chapters: This book grapples with the meaning of life and the fleeting nature of earthly pursuits. The author, often identified as Solomon, concludes with the importance of fearing God and keeping His commandments, finding ultimate meaning and satisfaction in a life lived in obedience to Him.

Song of Solomon Chapter Summaries

8 Chapters: This poetic work celebrates romantic love and intimacy within the context of marriage. Its allegorical interpretation can also be applied to the love between God and His people.

Isaiah Chapter Summaries

66 Chapters: This book, the longest in the Old Testament, contains powerful prophecies condemning Israel's sin and calling for repentance, while offering hope for future restoration and the coming Messiah. Isaiah emphasizes God's power, justice, and ultimate redemptive plan.

Jeremiah Chapter Summaries
52 Chapters: This book records the emotional and challenging ministry of Jeremiah, the weeping prophet, as he calls for repentance and warns of impending judgment for Judah's rebellion. Despite the dire pronouncements, Jeremiah also offers messages of hope and restoration.

Lamentations Chapter Summaries
5 Chapters: This book is a collection of five mournful poems lamenting the destruction of Jerusalem and the suffering of the people. It expresses deep sorrow and grief yet ultimately points to God's mercy and the hope for future restoration.

Ezekiel Chapter Summaries
48 Chapters: This book utilizes vivid imagery and symbolic actions to convey God's messages of judgment and hope to the Israelites in exile. Ezekiel emphasizes God's sovereignty and faithfulness even in the midst of judgment.

Daniel Chapter Summaries
12 Chapters: This book tells the stories of Daniel and his friends, faithful Jews who find success and favor in the Babylonian and Medo-Persian empires. Through dreams and visions, Daniel receives revelations about the future, including the rise and fall of empires and the coming Kingdom of God.

Hosea Chapter Summaries
14 Chapters: In this prophetic book, God uses the metaphor of a broken marriage to illustrate Israel's unfaithfulness and His own enduring love and desire for their restoration. Hosea emphasizes God's forgiveness and compassion.

Joel Chapter Summaries
3 Chapters: This book warns of impending judgment through a vivid description of a locust plague, while also offering a call to repentance and a promise of restoration for those who turn to God.

Amos Chapter Summaries
9 Chapters: This book criticizes the social injustices and religious hypocrisy within Israel, calling for a return to true justice and righteousness. Amos emphasizes God's concern for the poor and oppressed.

Obadiah Chapter Summary
1 Chapter: This shortest book in the Old Testament pronounces judgment on the nation of Edom for their lack of compassion toward Israel in its time of need.

Jonah Chapter Summaries
4 Chapters: This book tells the story of the prophet Jonah who initially disobeys God's call, only to be swallowed by a large fish and eventually fulfilling his mission to preach repentance to the city of Nineveh. It highlights God's mercy and compassion extending even to foreigners.

Micah Chapter Summaries
7 Chapters: This book echoes the messages of other prophets, condemning social injustice and religious hypocrisy while offering hope for a future ruler who will establish peace and justice.

Nahum Chapter Summaries
3 Chapters: This book pronounces judgment on the city of Nineveh, known for its cruelty and wickedness, but also offers a glimpse of hope for those who seek God.

Habakkuk Chapter Summaries
3 Chapters: This book presents a dialogue between the prophet Habakkuk and God, as the prophet grapples with the question of why God allows the wicked to prosper. He ultimately finds peace and trust in God's character and ultimate victory.

Zephaniah Chapter Summaries
3 Chapters: This book calls for repentance and warns of judgment for Judah's sin and idolatry. Yet, it also offers a message of hope for a remnant who will remain faithful and experience future restoration.

Haggai Chapter Summaries
2 Chapters: This book encourages the Israelites who returned from exile to

rebuild the Temple, highlighting the importance of obedience and faithfulness to God's commands.

Zechariah Chapter Summaries
14 Chapters: This book offers messages of hope and encouragement for the post-exilic community, containing symbolic visions and pronouncements about the coming Messiah and the future restoration of Jerusalem.

Malachi Chapter Summaries
4 Chapters: This book, the last in the Old Testament, critiques the religious complacency and moral failings of the people and calls for a return to faithfulness and worship of God. It concludes with a promise of the coming messenger (John the Baptist) and the return of Elijah.

End of the 39 Old Testament Book Summaries

Note:

NO, the Old Testament was absolutely NOT nailed to the cross with the man named Jesus. Just ask God Himself

May God bless us forever

Interesting ‘Torah Facts’

The phrase “lasting ordinance” is used 25 times in the Old Testament, in the Books of Moses. The word translated “lasting” is the Hebrew *olam*, meaning “forever” or “for a long time,” or ‘always,” or “perpetual”. God never says, “…or until …”. Forever is forever and has no end.

Hebrew	English
1 הפרק	**CHAPTER 1**
בראשית ברא אלהים את השמים ואת הארץ:	In the beginning God created the heaven and the earth.
2 והארץ היתה תהו ובהו וחשך על פני תהום ורוח אלהים מרחפת על פני המים:	2 And the earth was without form, and void; and darkness was upon the face of the deep. And the Spirit of God moved upon the face of the waters.
3 ויאמר אלהים יהי אור ויהי אור:	3 And God said, Let there be light: and there was light.
4 וירא אלהים את האור כי טוב ויבדל אלהים בין האור ובין החשך:	4 And God saw the light, that it was good: and God divided the light from the darkness.
5 ויקרא אלהים לאור יום ולחשך קרא לילה ויהי ערב ויהי בקר יום אחד:	5 And God called the light Day, and the darkness he called Night. And the evening and the morning were the first day.
6 ויאמר אלהים יהי רקיע בתוך המים ויהי מבדיל בין מים למים:	6 And God said, Let there be a firmament in the midst of the waters, and let it divide the waters from the waters.
7 ויעש אלהים את הרקיע ויבדל בין המים אשר מתחת לרקיע ובין המים אשר מעל לרקיע ויהי כן:	7 And God made the firmament, and divided the waters which were under the firmament from the waters which were above the firmament: and it was so.
8 ויקרא אלהים לרקיע שמים ויהי ערב ויהי בקר יום שני:	8 And God called the firmament Heaven. And the evening and the morning were the second day.
9 ויאמר אלהים יקוו המים מתחת השמים אל מקום אחד ותראה היבשה ויהי כן:	9 And God said, Let the waters under the heaven be gathered together unto one place, and let the dry land appear: and it was so.
10 ויקרא אלהים ליבשה ארץ ולמקוה המים קרא ימים וירא אלהים כי טוב:	10 And God called the dry land Earth; and the gathering together of the waters called he Seas: and God saw that it was good.

What is the Torah?
The Torah is a central reference of the religious Judaic tradition. It contains foundational narratives, laws, and teachings. Here are some fascinating facts about this ancient text.

01 The Torah consists of five books: Genesis, Exodus, Leviticus, Numbers, and Deuteronomy.

02 The word "Torah" means "instruction" or "teaching" in Hebrew.

03 It is also known as the Pentateuch, derived from the Greek words for "five books."

04 The Torah is written in Hebrew, the ancient language of the Jewish people.

05 It is traditionally handwritten on a scroll made from kosher animal parchment.

06 The Torah was given to Moses on Mount Sinai according to Jewish tradition.

07 It has been read and studied for over 3,000 years.

08 The Dead Sea Scrolls, discovered in the 20th century, include some of the oldest known copies of the Torah.

09 The Torah has influenced many other religious texts, including the Christian Old Testament.

10 Jewish communities around the world read the entire Torah in a yearly cycle, known as the Torah reading cycle.

11 Genesis covers the creation of the world and the early history of humanity.

12 Exodus tells the story of the Israelites' enslavement in Egypt and their subsequent liberation.

13 Leviticus focuses on laws and religious rituals.

14 Numbers recounts the Israelites' journey through the desert.

15 Deuteronomy consists of speeches by Moses, reiterating the laws for the new generation.

16 During synagogue services, the Torah is read from a special platform called a bimah.

17 The Torah scroll is adorned with a decorative cover, often embroidered with symbols and texts.

18 A yad, a pointer, is used to follow the text during reading to avoid touching the parchment.

19 On Simchat Torah, a Jewish holiday, the completion of the annual Torah reading cycle is celebrated with dancing and singing.

20 Bar and Bat Mitzvah ceremonies often involve reading from the Torah, marking a young person's coming of age.

21 Many Jewish families have a Torah scroll or a printed version in their homes.

22 Torah study is a lifelong pursuit for many Jews, with study groups and classes available in many communities.

23 The Torah has been translated into numerous languages, making its teachings accessible to a global audience.

24 Digital versions of the Torah are available, allowing for study and reading on electronic devices.

25 The principles and ethics found in the Torah continue to influence modern legal systems and moral philosophies.

26 The Torah's teachings on justice, charity, and community service inspire many social justice movements today.

The Torah isn't just a religious text; it's a cornerstone of Jewish culture and history. From its five books to the 613 commandments, the Torah offers a deep well of wisdom and guidance.
Its traditions and written laws have shaped countless lives and continue to influence modern society. Whether you're interested in its historical context, spiritual teachings, or cultural impact, the Torah provides a rich tapestry of knowledge. Understanding these 26 facts above, can give you a better appreciation of its significance. So next time you hear about the Torah, you'll know it's more than just a book; it's a living, breathing document that has stood the test of time. Dive into its teachings, and you might find something that resonates with you.

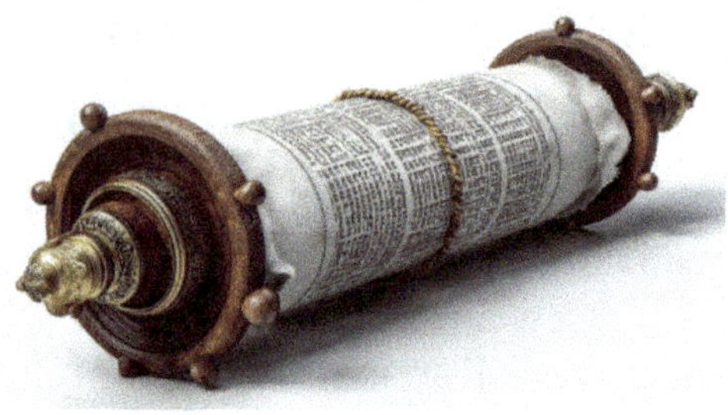

Torah Scroll & Hebrew Language Facts

The Torah is a sacred Jewish text written by hand on parchment by a specially trained scribe (sofer), taking about a year, and is incredibly precise, with 304,805 letters, where even one mistake invalidates the scroll. It has no vowels or punctuation and is read right-to-left, representing both written and oral traditions, acting as life's "instructions".

Ancient (Biblical) Hebrew differed fundamentally in their alphabet, writing direction, and grammatical structure. The most immediate differences were that Hebrew uses a 22-consonant alphabet written from right to left without vowels and consonants, while Modern English uses a 26-letter alphabet, with both vowels and consonants, written from left to right. **Ancient Hebrew had no capital letters, sentences, paragraphs, punctuation or vowels.** Ancient Hebrew is a much older language than English.

1. Ancient Hebrew was a combination of different dialects and was used in ancient Israel during the period between 10th century BC and fourth century AD. Modern Hebrew on the other hand has evolved as a common language of the Israel people.
2. Modern Hebrew is mainly based on the Sephardic Hebrew style.
3. In the Ancient Hebrew language, tense had no importance and there was no past, present and future. But in Modern Hebrew there is clear distinction of the three tenses "‘ past, present and future.
4. In ancient Hebrew a sentence began with a verb whereas in Modern Hebrew, the sentence starts with a

Subject which is generally followed by the verb and the object.

• A Torah Scroll is the holiest book within Judaism, made up of the five books of Moses.

• There are 304,805 letters in a Torah Scroll.

• Each page has 42 lines.

• The Torah Scroll must be written by a specially trained pious scribe called a *sofer*.

• A *sofer* must know more than 4,000 Judaic laws before he begins writing a Torah Scroll.

• It takes about a year to write an entire Torah Scroll.

• Even a single missing or misshapen letter invalidates the entire Sefer Torah.

• The Torah we use today in your synagogue is written exactly the same way the Torah was
written the very first time by Moses 3,300 years ago.

• The Torah is made of many sheets of parchment that are sewn together to make one very long scroll.

• The entire Torah is written by hand, each letter is inscribed and individually formed with a quill and specially prepared ink.

• The Torah is read at least four times a week in synagogues around the world.

• In Temple times, the king would read aloud from the Torah during the Hakhel gatherings.

Torah Trivia

For these questions, you will need to refer to the complete version of the Torah to answer.

GENESIS

1) Who was the first man to build a city? **Genesis 4:17**
2) What is the significance of the rainbow? **Genesis 9:12-17**
3) Who is the first priest mentioned in the Bible? **Genesis 14:18**
4) Who is the first prophet mentioned in the Bible? **Genesis 20:7**
5) What Old Testament figure's name means "laughter"? ***Genesis 21:3-6***
6) Who saw a heavenly ladder with the Lord standing above it? **Genesis 28:10-13**
7) Which of Jacob's wives was the first to bear children? **Genesis 29:31-32**

EXODUS

1) What river was turned to blood? **Exodus 7:20**
2) When the plague of hail came on the Egyptians, where was the one place it did not fall? **Exodus 9:26**
3) What stopped the plague of locusts in Egypt? **Exodus 10:19**
4) What did the Israelites put on their doorframes so the angel of death would pass over? **Exodus 12:21-23**
5) How did the bitter water of Marah become sweet? **Exodus 15:23-25**
6) What mountain did the Lord descend upon in fire? **Exodus 19:18**
7) What idol did the Israelites worship in the wilderness? **Exodus 32:4-6**

LEVITICUS

1) According to the law, what could be used in place of a lamb as a sin offering? **Leviticus 5:7**
2) Who did Moses anoint with the blood of a ram? **Leviticus 8:23**
3) After the consecration of Aaron and his sons, what consumed the offering on the altar? **Leviticus 9:22-24**
4) What two sons of Aaron were devoured by fire for offering unauthorized fire before the Lord? **Leviticus 10:1-2**
5) What portable object did the cloud of God's glory appear over? **Leviticus *16:2***
6) What was the punishment for committing adultery? **Leviticus 20:10**
7) What kind of animals were not to be sacrificed to God? **Leviticus 22:22**

NUMBERS

1) What color was the cloth over the altar in the tabernacle? Numbers 4:11
2) Why didn't Moses give any tabernacle offerings to the Kohathites? Numbers 7:9
4) What two men tore their clothes when the Israelites murmured against the Lord about going into Canaan? Numbers 14:6
5) Where did Aaron die? Numbers 20:25-29
6) What sinister creatures did God send to kill many of the Israelites in the desert? Numbers 21:6
7) What leader fashioned a bronze snake? Numbers 21:9
8) What did the talking donkey say to Balaam? Numbers 22:28-30

DEUTERONOMY

1)Who had a huge bed made of iron? Deuteronomy 3:11
2) What is the first commandment with promise? Deuteronomy 5:16
3) According to the law, how many witnesses were necessary before a person could be tried and put to death? Deuteronomy 17:6
4) According to the law, what were the Israelites to do if they found a mother bird with young or with eggs? Deuteronomy 22:6-7
5) What were the best-made shoes in the Bible? Deuteronomy 29:5
6) What mountain did Moses see the Promised Land from? Deuteronomy 34:1-4
7) Who buried Moses? Deuteronomy 34:5-6

Reference for Resources Used

~~~~~~

1. Berlin, Adele, and Marc Zvi Brettler, eds. The Jewish Study Bible. (Print) (Reference Publication)
2. Freedman, David Noel, ed. The Anchor Yale Bible Dictionary. (Print) (Encyclopedia)
3. Metzger, Bruce M., and Michael D. Coogan, eds. The Oxford Companion to the Bible. (Print) (Reference Publication)
4. Sakenfeld, Katharine Doob, ed. The New Interpreter's Dictionary of the Bible. (Print) (Encyclopedia)
5. VanGemeren, Willem A., ed. New International Dictionary of Old Testament Theology & Exegesis. (Print) (Reference Publication)
6. TheTrueNameTorah, TorahPublications .com
7. LearnBibleDaily .com
8. EnterTheBible .org
9. FreeBibleStudyHub .com
10. EverGrowingChristians .com/
11. BibleVise .com
12. TruthSaves .org
13. The Jewish Study Bible
14. The Oxford Handbook of Biblical Studies
15. The New Interpreter's Dictionary of the Bible
16. The Oxford Dictionary of the Jewish Religion
17. Dictionary of Deities and Demons in the Bible
18. The Oxford Companion to the Bible
19. The Anchor Yale Bible Dictionary
20. Harper's Bible Dictionary
21. Dictionary of Deities and Demons in the Bible
22. The New Bible Dictionary
23. The True name Torah

Copyright © 2025-26 Torah Publications All Rights Reserved
~~~~~~

About the Author

YoHanan is a motivational speaker, life coach, and pastoral counselor with extensive experience in helping individuals navigate life's complexities and discover their life's purpose. He holds a Degree in Human Resource Management and Business Management and has 25 years of experience working with diverse populations. YoHanan's unique blend of pastoral care, coaching, and writing expertise has enabled him to create a practical and compassionate guide for readers seeking to live a more fulfilling and meaningful life. He is also a published author of 40 Days of AHA! Moments with God on the Mountain, The True Name Torah, Why Did Man Change God's Sabbath, What God Wants You to Know, and If you Knew God Like I Know God. All of these are available at Amazon.com, by title.

His Hobbies are woodworking and writing motivational material. He lives in Texas with his wife raising their two granddaughters. He has lived in Pennsylvania, Ohio, Florida, Kenitra Morocco, Nantucket Island, California and Texas. He served four years in the US Navy and is a Viet Nam era veteran.

Other Books from this author are available by Title at Amazon.com

The True Name Torah, God's Name Restored

Beyond the Shrouded Mountain

40 Days of AHA Moments With God

Why Did Man Change God's Sabbath

If You Knew God Like I Know God

What God Wants You To Know

www.ingramcontent.com/pod-product-compliance
Lightning Source LLC
LaVergne TN
LVHW061224100826
845148LV00004B/855

* 9 7 8 1 7 3 4 5 3 8 3 5 9 *